An Ember Still Glowing

AN EMBER STILL GLOWING

Humankind as the Image of God

HARRY R. BOER

WILLIAM B. EERDMANS PUBLISHING COMPANY
GRAND RAPIDS, MICHIGAN

255 Jefferson Ave. S.E., Grand Rapids, Mich. 49503

Printed in the United States of America

Library of Congress Cataloging-in-Publication Data

Boer, Harry R.
An ember still glowing: humankind as the image of God /
Harry R. Boer.
p. cm.
ISBN 0-8028-0434-9
1. Man (Christian theology). 2. Image of God. 3. Election (Theology).
4. Reformed Church—Doctrines. I. Title.
BT701.2.B587 1990
233′.5—dc20 89-28098
CIP

To
the memory of

James Daane

Dear Friend
and
Theological Companion

Contents

Introduction

The present book has grown out of theological reflection on my thirty-six years of ecumenical ministry. This period covers three and a half years in the military chaplaincy during World War II and twenty-six years of missionary service in Nigeria, chiefly in pastoral training. These years were interspersed with six years of postgraduate study in schools as diverse as Westminster Theological Seminary, the Free University of Amsterdam, Union Theological Seminary in New York, and the University of Chicago Divinity School and with one year of seminary teaching in missiology in the United States. I received my basic theological education at Calvin Theological Seminary in Grand Rapids, Michigan. My doctoral work I did in Amsterdam.

In my work of training pastors, I taught students from churches that had risen out of Methodist, Church of the Brethren, Baptist, Lutheran, Anglican, Plymouth Brethren, Reformed, Evangelical and United Brethren, and undenominational missions. The work involved me in educational, administrative, and religious fellowship with teachers in the Theological College of Northern Nigeria from all these traditions.

My retirement in 1978 gave me opportunity to assess where I had come to stand theologically in relation to my own Reformed tradition and to the other fellowships with which I had lived and served. It seemed to me that to make this assessment I should have a basic starting point that is dominantly significant in its own right while not being distinctive of any particular theological tradition. This I found in the common Christian teaching of the creation of Man* in the image of God.

Belief in this teaching undergirds not only our common Christian faith. The fact of our creation as *imago Dei* is also the basis of mankind's common humanity. By image of God I do not mean some characteristic or quality human beings have in common with God, so that every person can be said to be "an image of God." Rather, I see mankind—the whole of mankind, past, present, and future, male and female, old and young, every race of Man, and as an organic unit—to constitute the one image of God. In this one mighty and varied human entity, all women and men participate. They participate in it, however, under the condition of sin. The bright flame of its original image is now only an ember, but an ember still glowing. And it is in the service of this universal human wholeness in all its fragile greatness and all its pervasive evil that the saving work of Christ the divine-human *imago Dei* involves us.

How do the ramifications of such a conception affect our understanding of the work of God in Man's salvation? The pages that follow test basic Reformed teachings by this standard. I have found again and again that these teachings do not in fact stand up under examination. Still, this should not lead us to reject them as outcasts from the body of Reformed theology. They have served too long and often too fruitfully simply to be rejected. Rather, they have been overtaken as stages in the development of doctrine and as such must be replaced. This involves a certain emancipation from doctrines still professed but no longer gen-

*It is unfortunate that the English language does not have a gender-neutral monosyllabic name for humanity, as in the Dutch *Mens* and the German *Mensch*. In the necessarily frequent reference to mankind I have used the shorter word "Man," trusting that its capitalization will lift it above the gender reference to the level of humankind.

uinely confessed in the ongoing faith and life of the church of Christ in its Reformed expression. But such emancipation, when truly lived and practiced, becomes a renewed commitment to the tradition, which far from being surrendered is enriched and made more fruitful.

I have not considered it my duty to suggest how other theological traditions in the Christian church could benefit from a similar reevaluation. Only one who has lived deeply with her or his own church's body of doctrine theologically, practically, and personally can undertake such a task. This is not to say that the present essay cannot stimulate others to ask whether the basic concept of mankind as *imago Dei* has implications for other theological understandings of the gospel. My hope, indeed, is that it will encourage such inquiry.

—Harry R. Boer

Chapter I

Man in the Structure of Existence

Then God said, "Let us make man in our image, after our likeness." . . . So God created man in his own image, in the image of God he created him; male and female he created them.

Genesis 1:26-27

The glory of Man is that he is the image and likeness of God. He is not an angel, he is not an animal, he is not a thing. He is person. She is person. Both are equally and complementarily person. Man acts today, he is accountable for yesterday, he plans for tomorrow. He uses time to schedule all that he does. The whole world is his to examine, to use, to enjoy, and to develop. Nowhere is he forbidden entrance, whether in the landmass of the earth, in the depths of the ocean, or in the heights of the heavens. Matter, plant and animal life, even formless space acknowledge his superiority. He is lord of all his environing world.

Even so, Man's dominion over all these dimensions of creation is a qualified dominion. He can fruitfully exercise power over them only when he acknowledges the profound interrelationships between him and the other-than-human aspects of the vast environment he is given in which to live his life. His relationship to them is utterly intimate and organic. The earth is his habitat without which he cannot exist. The air that he breathes, the food he eats, the water he drinks are the *sine qua non* of his existence. To manage his environment well is not only an inborn task but also a matter of self-interest.

Not the least part of his mandate is to understand the created character of the mute creation and the "rights" which this gives it in relation to him. Through the telescope he scans the sun and the moon and the stars, and through his microscope he examines minute animal life and elements of matter. He searches out the meaning of things. The world without Man is incomplete, but Man without the world is inconceivable. And both Man and world live and move and have their being in God alone.

Both Man's headship over and dependence upon the world arise directly from his status as creature made in the image of God. He is master of all he surveys and therefore stands over it; he is an organic part of what he surveys and therefore stands under himself. The stewardship given to Man in creation is first and foremost a stewardship of self. Performing that task well is the indispensable condition of successfully administering all things outside himself. The equipment given Man to discharge this dual office is inherent in the distinctive character of his being: made "in the image and likeness of God."

Although theologians through the centuries have puzzled over the distinction between "image" and "likeness," no convincing answer has been found. The use of "likeness" is best understood as stating in a different way, and thus emphasizing, the fact of Man's being imaged after God—as we might say that "Martha is the image, the very likeness, of her mother."

Far wider attention has been given to what is meant by the expression "image of God." In particular, what is the nature of the image of God as it manifests itself in the historical period between the fall of Man in paradise and the reconstitution of all things in the new heaven and the new earth?

The effort to understand what is meant by the image of God under the condition of sin faces the obstacle that the creation account in Genesis provides only very limited data describing Man in the state of innocence, making comparison difficult. Nevertheless, what is said about the *imago Dei* before the fall is basic to understanding the image of God in the state of sin. An exploration of the given witness suggests a number of illuminating perspectives:

In the first creation account (Gen. 1:1–2:4) the creation of Man is given a format that is altogether unique. Each preceding creative act has been introduced by an impersonal construction: "Let there be light," "Let there be a firmament," "Let the earth put forth," etc. The creation of Man also arises out of a divine "Let . . ." but with a notable difference: "*Let us make Man* in our image, after our likeness."

Here is reflected a prior divine deliberation that does not characterize any of the other creative acts, which seem to have been brought forth as a spontaneous response to the "Let . . ." command alone. In the creation of Man there is a consultative divine decision to "make Man" not only as a living entity by himself simply, but also "in our image, after our likeness."

All other living creatures called into being are called as whole classes of varied life: vegetation, plants, swarms of living creatures, birds, sea monsters, cattle, creeping things, beasts of the earth, and all these "according to their kind." Although animal life is sexually constituted, only of Man is this specifically stated: "male and female he created them." Like other creatures, they must "be fruitful and multiply."

In two other respects Man stands apart. He will have "dominion" over all living things, and he must "subdue" the earth. He is the apex of God's creative work, not only because of his greater complexity, specifically as image and likeness of the Creator, but because, being thus made, he will be God's vicar, as governor, steward, and developer of the earth and all that is in it.

There appears to be an intimate relation between the image in which Man was created and the work he was given to do. Just as "image" relates Man to God as personal being, so the commands to exercise dominion and to subdue the earth relate Man directly to God's creational work. *God the prototype* created; *Man the image* governs the created world. And similarly, God the prototype *created;* man the image *governs.* Prototype and image, creation and governance—these are basic correspondences that bear on the meaning of Man as the image of God.

The task given will make such demands on Man's ability, wisdom, and ingenuity that it is no overstatement to say that Man, being made in the image of the Creator, becomes himself a creating agent. Provided that the image is willing to remain image and does not arrogate to itself the power and ultimacy of the Prototype, it is helpful to say that Man as image is an imaged creator, *homo sapiens* and *homo faber*—Man the intelligent being and Man the maker of things.

The second creation account (Gen. 2:4b-25) illustrates the relation of Man as image of God to the Creator by his being placed in the garden of Eden "to till it and keep it." What God has *made* must be *maintained.* As in the first account, the once-for-all act of creating is given continuing existence by the involvement of Man's concern and labor.

Genesis 2 goes on to exemplify Man's dominion over the world in a particular instance. God brought to him "every beast of the field and every bird of the air" to see what he would call them, "and whatever the man called every living creature, that was its name" (Gen. 2:19).

This was a most remarkable challenge for Adam, for Semitic culture did not understand a name as a sort of convenient identification tag but as a signification of the inner essence of the entity named. This is the background of the prohibition "You shall not take the name of the Lord your God in vain" (Exod. 20:7). It is expressed in the angelic instruction to Joseph, "You shall call his name Jesus, for he will save his people from their sins" (Matt. 1:21).

The naming of the animals served the further purpose of causing Adam to sense his aloneness, and God found occasion to satisfy his desire by meeting an existential need. This in turn occasioned another naming ceremony on Adam's part: "She shall be called Woman, because she was taken out of Man" (Gen. 2:23).

Note the remarkable correspondence between the mandate of stewardship given to Man and the nature of the world that he is to govern. The act of creation from pre-existent substance which was "without form and void" was in fact the transforming of chaos into cosmos by the structuration of matter according to physical laws. The laws involved are as much and as wonderful a part of the creation as are the physical structures—minute, small, large, or stupendous—which they fashion and undergird. It is an essential part of Man's dominion over and stewardship of the earth to search out, understand, and apply these laws for his own benefit and for that of the environing world in which he lives.

Further, we need not depend exclusively on Scripture to understand what the image of God in Man is. When St. Paul declares that what can be known about God is plain to men, "because God has shown it to them. Ever since the creation of the world his invisible nature, namely, his eternal power and deity, has been clearly perceived in the things that have been made" (Rom. 1:19-20), he is reasoning from the creation to the Creator, from the thing made to the Maker. Perceiving God's eternal power and deity from the mountains and the brooks and the stars is not simply an objective, rational deduction. It is a conclusion that is natively induced in Man by his being made in the image of God.

Between the true image and the Prototype there is a fellowship, a mutuality, in which each recognizes himself in the other. This recognition is not simply rational, however rational it may be. It is not merely heartfelt, however much hearts may be intertwined. As Man came forth from the hand of God, he was truly "by nature" religious. That sin suppresses this knowledge in the sinner in no way excuses the absence of the recognition the works of God should constantly elicit.

One may thus ask whether it is not only permissible but even necessary to reason from the phenomenon of Man (in terms of the mutuality suggested above) to his Creator and thus gain insight into the character of the Prototype in order better to understand oneself as image. Jesus said, "He who has seen me has seen the Father; how can you say, 'Show us the Father'?" (John 14:9). Is this not in some measure also true of those who are conformed to the image of his Son (Rom. 8:29)? Is it not true even of those who are not in Christ but reveal in their words and deeds something of the wisdom and power of the Creator? Is there anyone to whom it is inappropriate to say, "What have you that you did not receive?" (1 Cor. 4:7). And if someone manifests an excellent or praiseworthy quality (Phil. 4:8), shall we not see in this a reflection of God's goodness and a revelation of his excellence?

We should also note God's own evaluation of his creative work: "And God saw everything that he had made, and behold, it was very good" (Gen. 1:31). As he brought the various segments of the envisioned whole into being, he declared six times "and it was so"; five times he expressed the judgment that "it was good." In these words we discern a massively determinative quality of God's creative work in its unbroken integrity. The words "good" and especially "very good" encapsulate such ideas as fitness, appropriateness, adequacy, suitability for achieving the purpose it is intended to serve. And there are not least the affective qualities of love, sympathy, kindness, and understanding, as in the reminiscence "Mother was so *good* to us." God brought into being a partner, a companion, a friend with whom he could have dialogue and fellowship. He did this on a scale as vast and grand as the concepts image and creation could conceivably permit: he made Man to be co-divine to the limits of the possible, against the background of an infinitely complex and beautiful macro-microcosmic environment. Such was Man when he trod the new-formed earth—Man the image of God, God's very own and beloved *alter ego.*

The image that God created was *one,* not two which by the reproductive process could become many. When Adam and Eve were brought into being, they were not each an image of God. As individuals they were male and female. As a oneness they constituted *mankind.* They were *humanity.* Genesis 1:26-27 reports, "Let us make *man* in our image . . . so God created *man* in his own image, in the image of God he created *him*; male and female he created *them.*" We do well always to understand that according to the biblical picture there is only *one* image of God. This expressed itself first in two people, husband and wife, who by reproduction constituted a family out of which grew other families, then clans, tribes, nations, races. But always when few became many and many became thousands and thousands became millions, there was always one, and only one, *imago Dei.*

In that one image all human beings *participate.* But this participation means exactly what it says: all reflect one image, which like a tree producing ever more branches and foliage does not cease to be one and the same tree. It is the fact of participation in the one image of God that makes her, that makes him, a human being. But there is only one humanity which is the image of God. No one person is or has ever been *the* image of God. Only mankind, whether as two or as many, is *imago Dei.*

Though generations may come and go and tribes and nations cease to exist, God always and everywhere has an imaged partner to address and by whom to be addressed. It is, of course, always a partial image that God addresses and by whom he is addressed. That part of the image which no longer is and that which is yet to be born, together with that now existing, alike await the great reconstitution of all things when the image envisaged from eternity shall stand before God in the completeness of all its parts and he shall be everything to everyone (1 Cor. 15:28).[1]

What the image of God essentially *is* has intrigued theologians over the centuries. No common understanding has emerged from this preoccupation. Since a detailed exposition of these various viewpoints would be tedious, we will limit ourselves here to a brief indication of them.

It has been suggested that the *imago* consists in Man's memory, intellect, and love (reflecting the three persons of the trinity); or in the moral character of unfallen Man as reflecting

1. New International Version has "that God may be all in all."

the purity of God; or in Man's freedom as a spiritual being; or in the capacity for fellowship with God; or in true knowledge, righteousness, and holiness; or that the *imago* is a symbol of the principle of historical development. About all such understandings Karl Barth has made a trenchant observation:

> We might easily discuss which of these and the many other similar explanations is the finest and deepest and most serious. What we cannot discuss is which of them is the true explanation of Gen. 1:26. For it is obvious that their authors merely found the concept [of image] in the text and then proceeded to pure invention in accordance with the requirements of contemporary anthropology.[2]

At this point we are not dealing with either the impoverishment or the redemption of the image. We are concerned solely with the nature of *that* entity which came unblemished out of the hand of the Creator and was therefore declared to be "very good." Inevitably, then, we must draw the meaning of "image" from Genesis 1:26-31, for all other references in Scripture to Man as image or likeness of God are in the context of sin or redemption or both. The image in which Man was created had neither of these as contextual elements.

It is my personal judgment that the central characteristic of Man as image of God is the quality of personhood. It is characteristic of God as sole Deity, and it is equally and radically distinctive of the three members of the trinity. Personhood is, differently but in the same measure, characteristic of the female and the male members of the human species, of which fact Barth takes prominent note when he underscores the Scripture's "So God created man in his own image, in the image of God he created him; *male and female he created them.*"[3] Neither male nor female can come into being without the other, and each con-

2. Karl Barth, *Church Dogmatics,* Vol. 3, Pt. 1: *Doctrine of Creation, the Work of Creation*, ed. and trans. G. W. Bromiley and T. F. Torrance (Edinburgh: T. & T. Clark, 1958), p. 193.

3. Barth, *Church Dogmatics*, pp. 184-87.

tributes a particular quality to the family and to society as a whole. It is personhood that distinguishes Man from the higher animals. It is personhood that makes possible both the eminence of genius in particular human beings and the common qualities that characterize members of any given culture, distinguishing it from all others.

With these considerations as background, we can say that God created Man to exist *in a structure of relationships.* Formally this structure is *unchangeable.* Materially it is *altogether* changeable. In creating Man, God placed him in four basic and enduring relationships: to God, to fellowman, to the world around him, and to himself.

In the beginning these relationships were "very good." There was disruption neither in the religious, nor in the social, nor in the environmental spheres. There was a blessed concord between the Creator and his creation; and within the creation all levels of existence functioned according to their respective given characters. Man was responsibly subject to God; he was in fellowship with the neighbor as his equal; he was steward over the natural world; he was at peace with himself. Within this pattern of relationships he was free to work out the potential within him, namely, to achieve, within the bounds of human finitude, what his existence in the image of God required of him.

This universal rapport was broken by Man's fall into sin, precisely in the basic areas in which it had prevailed before the fall. In the religious area: "the man and his wife hid themselves from the presence of the Lord God" (Gen. 3:8); in the social: "the woman whom thou gavest to be with me, she gave me fruit of the tree, and I ate" (3:12); in the environmental: "cursed is the ground because of you; . . . thorns and thistles it shall bring forth to you" (3:17b, 18); in the personal: guilt and insecurity beset him (4:13-16). Sin basically altered the quality of the creationally given *relationships,* yet in such a manner that the creationally given *structure of existence* within which they came to expression remained unchanged.

The stars in their courses, day and night, the seasons, the fish and birds and animals pursuing their instinctive habits, with Man still the dominant figure—all this continued. But the *goodness* was out of it. In the sweat of his face the man now ate his bread, in pain the woman brought forth children, and both would return to the dust from which they had been taken (Gen. 3:16-19). The wolf no longer dwelt with the lamb, the leopard no longer lay down with the kid, and a little child no longer led them (Isa. 11:6). Existence went on, but relationships entered upon irresoluble disarray. St. Paul would put the consequences vividly: "We know that the whole creation has been groaning in travail together until now" (Rom. 8:22).

Nevertheless, God continued to regard Man as made in his image. He will require a life for a life of Man when he sheds human blood, "for God made man in his own image" (Gen. 9:5-6). So imposing is what remains of the image of God in Man that the psalmist sees him as made little less than God, who has crowned him with glory and honor (Ps. 8:5).

So deeply is this relationship engraved in the Judeo-Christian tradition that the writers of its Scriptures did not hesitate to apply to God typically human activities and capacities: judge, king, father, counselor, husbandman, shepherd, teacher, leader of a host. In his Gospel, Luke speaks of Adam as "the son of God" (3:38); Paul approvingly quotes a pagan poet: "for we are indeed his offspring" (Acts 17:28). He exhorts his readers to put on "the new nature, created after the likeness of God in true righteousness and holiness" (Eph. 4:24), and, similarly, "the new nature, which is being renewed in knowledge after the image of its creator" (Col. 3:10). Warning against the destructive use of the tongue, James writes, "With it we bless the Lord and Father, and with it we curse men, who are made in the likeness of God" (3:9).

These references, though few, are clear-cut. Despite his sin, Man remains the image of God. These relatively infrequent explicit references to Man as image of God provide the positive ground for the doctrine of the *imago Dei.* Another, larger group of biblical passages set forth the image relationship in terms of "as" and "as-so." Of the many references the following are typical: "As a father pities his children, so the Lord pities those who fear him" (Ps. 103:13); "You, therefore, must be perfect, as your heavenly Father is perfect" (Matt. 5:48); "Be kind to one another, tenderhearted, forgiving one another, as God in Christ forgave you" (Eph. 4:32); "Therefore be imitators of God, as beloved children" (Eph. 5:1); "As he who called you is holy, be holy yourselves in all your conduct; since it is written, 'You shall be holy, for I am holy' " (1 Pet. 1:15-16).

This pronounced Father-child relationship between God and believers can hardly be viewed as other than a human, affective casting of the God-image relationship. Although these passages describe the relationship of *believers* to God, this does not exclude those who stand outside of Christ from the God-image comparison. To the children of the heavenly Father it applies redemptively as well as by creation; to others it applies by virtue of creation alone. As will become clearer later, the fact that people can be called out of darkness to God's marvelous light is grounded precisely in their participation in the universal image of God, which makes them able to respond to his call.

In support of the specific references to and eloquent intimations of Man as image of God, we should note the often familiar interaction between God and Man in terms of friendship, intimacy, and concern. The Lord spoke to Moses "face to face, as a man speaks to his friend" (Exod. 33:11). Abraham was God's friend (2 Chron. 20:7; Jas. 2:23). God is close to the brokenhearted and saves those who are crushed in spirit (Ps. 34:18); he is near to all who call on him (Isa. 50:8); he is not far from each one of us (Acts 17:27); Enoch walked with God (Gen. 5:22); God's covenant with Levi was a covenant of life and peace, and he walked with God in peace and uprightness (Mal. 2:5-6).

Indeed, just as Man as image of God becomes through faith partaker "of the divine nature" (2 Pet. 1:4), so the scriptural witness to God's faithfulness, constancy, love, patience, sternness, justice, comfort, peace, joy, and fellowship makes it reasonable to speak in some sense of God's "humanity." This is particularly evident if we consider that it is creation in the image of God, and that *alone,* which makes Man *human.*

The climactic scriptural witness to Man as the image of God is the incarnation of the Word of God in Jesus of Nazareth. He, the Son of God, the image of the invisible God, through whom and for whom all things were created (Col. 1:15-17), became flesh and dwelt among us (John 1:14), to become within our history the visible external human image of the Father. All that he is and says and does flows not from his own authority, "but the Father who dwells in me does his works." Whoever has seen him has seen the Father (John 14:9-11). Jesus' being in human form is the wholly adequate vehicle to reflect his Father's character and work. Who can doubt his full and unqualified humanity? Born of a woman (Gal. 4:4), he grew up obedient to his parents, increasing in wisdom and stature and held in favor by God and men (Luke 2:51-52). He was tempted like us in every respect, yet without sin (Heb. 2:18; 4:15). He was crucified, died, and was buried, according to the apostolic witness.

St. Paul marvelously rolls into one the pre-existent Son, who is the image of the invisible God in whom all things were created, and Christ incarnate, the head of the body, the church, who made peace between God and Man by the blood of the cross (Col. 1:15-20). Only the eye of faith can see this image, for the god of this world has blinded the minds of unbelievers so that they are unable to see the light of the glory of Christ, who is the likeness of God (2 Cor. 4:4). To this image, the glory of which was recognizable even in his earthly life (John 1:14), the believer is destined to be conformed (Rom. 8:29). The renewal of the image of God in Man therefore takes place through and in its renewal in the image of Christ the Redeemer. The comprehensiveness of the image-concept is thereby enlarged and deepened by a dimension wholly absent in the image represented by Adam in the state of innocence.

Our concern with Man as the image of God may not obscure the fact that it is not only in Man that God's being and majesty and power are mirrored. There is a witness to God in the *whole* of his creation. The heavens are telling the glory of God, and the firmament proclaims his handiwork (Ps. 19:1). God's name is excellent in all the earth (Ps. 8:9), and his invisible nature is clearly evident in the things that have been made (Rom. 1:19-20). The Scriptures frequently present such testimony to the glory of God in the world, and for those who have eyes to see, the astounding discoveries of science confirm and comment on the biblical witness.

St. Augustine accompanied his discussion of the image of God with references to the natural world and its surrounding universe, which he called *vestigia Dei.* This expression has the pregnant meaning of "footsteps of God." In the sun and the moon and the stars in their galaxies, in the forests and the mountains and the oceans, in the rivers and the plains and all their teeming bird and fish and animal and insect life, Man finds a God-ward-pointing environment in the universal macro-micro entity called "the footsteps of God." *Vestigia* is the plural of the Latin word *vestigium,* meaning the sole of the foot, footprint, sign, token, or trace. When one *investigates* a matter, he follows its footprints or traces to discover its meaning. The English word *vestige* is derived from *vestigium,* and its general meaning is "something which remains after the destruction or disappearance of the main portion." But that is hardly its meaning in St. Augustine's use of it.

In *The Image of God: The Doctrine of St. Augustine and Its Influence,* John Edward Sullivan, O.P., sets forth Augustine's theological understanding of the term.[4] In all sentient life including Man and in all non-sentient existence he discovers clear traces not only of god as a unitary Principle, but of God as Trinity, that

4. John E. Sullivan, *The Image of God: The Doctrine of St. Augustine and Its Influence* (Dubuque, IA: Priory Press, 1963), pp. 84-93. Sullivan has seventy-seven footnotes to the third chapter, which is entitled "Vestiges of the Trinity." The large majority of these refer to Book 11 of St. Augustine's work *De Trinitate.* Nevertheless, he writes in footnote 18, "Despite the profuse use of the expression 'vestigia Trinitatis' by later commentators, it is rarely found in the *De Trinitate.*" He may not have anticipated how much later generations would be intrigued by the beautiful religious correspondence between the concepts *imago Dei* and *vestigia Dei.*

It is unfortunate that Sullivan used the literal English derivative "vestiges" in the title of chapter 3 since in the common language *vestige* chiefly has the meaning of a "ruin" or "faint trace." "Footprints" would have been more meaningful.

is, as tri-une. God is always one, but never without his manifestation in triads. Augustine's favorite text in the Bible for this is St. Paul's "For from him and through him and to him are all things" (Rom. 11:36). For material reference he noted with particular fondness Wisdom of Solomon 11:20 in the Apocrypha, "He has disposed all things in measure, number and weight."

> From God, the Triune God, all triads are derived; from him is the beginning of existence, the principle of knowledge, the law of loving. From God all animals derive the nature by which they live, the power by which they sense, and the motion by which they are appetitive. From God all bodies derive the measure by which they subsist, the number by which they are beautified, and their weight by which they are ordered. Yet it is not that the Father made one part of creation, the Son another, and the Holy Spirit a third. Rather, the Father through the Son in the gift of the Holy Spirit made all things and each individual thing. Anything that exists partakes of three qualities: it is a particular thing, it is distinguished from other things by its own species, and it does not disobey the order of nature.

I am deeply impressed with the concept of *vestigia Dei.* I am less impressed by the manner in which St. Augustine works it out and supports it. It is thoroughly abstract at the identical point at which the Bible is thoroughly concrete.

> The heavens are telling the glory of God;
> and the firmament proclaims his handiwork.
> Day to day pours forth speech,
> and night to night declares knowledge. (Ps. 19:1-2)
>
> The heavens proclaim his righteousness;
> and all the peoples behold his glory. (Ps. 97:6)
>
> In past generations he allowed all the nations
> to walk in their own ways;
> yet he did not leave himself without witness,
> for he did good and gave you from heaven
> rains and fruitful seasons, satisfying
> your hearts with food and gladness. (Acts 14:16-17)

For what can be known about God is plain to them,
because God has shown it to them.
Ever since the creation of the world
his invisible nature, namely, his eternal
power and deity, has been clearly perceived
in the things that have been made.
So they are without excuse. (Rom. 1:19-20)

This is language that the simple can understand. Only the academically trained can understand St. Augustine's abstract triads, and even they would be moved more to admiration than to worship. Moreover, Augustine's theory does not always stand up under analysis and testing. Even Father Sullivan has doubts about the legitimacy of the triads. He writes: "The Trinity of Persons is not simply Three, but Three-in-One. Where is the unity of the Godhead expressed by the Trinitarian reflections of Augustine? . . . The formulae . . . express the triplicity but seem to be deficient in representing the unity of God."[5]

These strictures, however, do not in any way detract from or minimize the truth and value of Augustine's basic thesis that the whole of creation constitutes a mighty witness to God's creative work. What impresses one powerfully is the explicit designation of the natural world as a clear-cut revelation of God the Creator. As God's image in Man makes Man a religious being, so God's footprints in the physical universe lend to it a religious quality that elicits from Man, the *imago Dei,* admiration, praise, and worship. And this response gains in seriousness and becomes compounded with fear when we consider the growing preoccupation with the man-made pollution of the environment. Here Christian concern must not only see the growing threat to human well-being but rise in revulsion against the mindless desecration not of a bland impersonal "nature" but of the footprint evidence for God's esthetic sensitivity and his sustentative provision for Man's need. Here is a fundamental principle that should have a large and enduring place in the exposition of a theology of the environment.

5. Sullivan, *The Image of God,* p. 93.

The great Creator God passed by here and left his footprints in trailing galaxies of light and glory. The earth, the mountains, and the hills break forth into singing; the trees of the field clap their hands; "and it shall be to the Lord for a memorial, for an everlasting sign which shall not be cut off" (Isa. 55:12-13). In this passage the footprints of the Creator point to and rejoice in the work of the Redeemer. "How beautiful upon the mountains are the feet of him who brings good tidings, who publishes peace" (Isa. 52:7). Man the image of God lives in the surrounding beauty of the Creator's majesty and through its poetry ascribes glory to the Redeemer.

The imaging of the divine in Man and its reflection in the environing creation have a scriptural counterbalance which prevents divine immanence from degenerating into pantheism. The fact that the divine image-making takes place *below* the line that divides the Creator from the creature is reinforced by declarations of the radical uniqueness of God the Creator. Neither the *imago* nor the *vestigia* may ever become idols with a divinity of their own.

There is simply *none like God.* Moses sang of him as a savior of Israel from the Egyptian oppressor: "Who is like thee, O Lord, among the gods? Who is like thee, majestic in holiness, terrible in glorious deeds, doing wonders?" (Exod. 15:11). David praised him: "Thou art great, O Lord God . . . and there is no God besides thee" (2 Sam. 7:22). The psalmist asked, "Who among the heavenly beings is like the Lord . . . ? Who is mighty as thou art, O Lord, with thy faithfulness round about thee?" (Ps. 89:6, 8). Isaiah exclaims, "To whom then will you liken God . . . ? To whom then will you compare me, that I should be like him? says the Holy One" (40:18, 25).

The God immanent in Man and wonderfully pointed to by the mountains, the forests, the seas, the galactic immensities, and all things living is the transcendent one whom no human has seen or can see. He is the blessed and only sovereign, King of kings and Lord of lords, who alone has immortality and dwells in light unapproachable. Infinitely exalted above his creation, he indwells it wholly. He it is in whom we live and move and have our being, whose Spirit we cannot escape, whose presence we cannot flee, our unfailing Father in Christ, while ever remaining the Creator and Ruler of the universe.

Chapter II

The Primacy of Melchizedek

And Melchizedek king of Salem brought out bread and wine; he was priest of God Most High. And he blessed him and said,

Blessed be Abram by God Most High, maker of heaven and earth;
and blessed be God Most High, who has delivered your enemies into your hand!

And Abram gave him a tenth of everything.

Genesis 14:18-20

In discussing Man as image of God under the condition of sin, it is fundamental to remember that sin is not a part of Man's created being. It came into his life *after* the work of creation had been completed and declared *good* by the Creator. In its primordial innocence the image that God created was not an object of either curse or redemption. Man and the whole world and the universe he was given to live in were solely and exclusively objects of God's beneficent creative will and power. Having been created in and for innocence, Man *became* an object of curse and redemption after he *had become* a sinner.

Here again, the first three chapters of Genesis are decisive. Man was created good, but the goodness was conditioned on his observing the prohibition of eating fruit from the tree of the knowledge of good and evil. The temptation to eat "and be like God" confronted Man with the central issue of his life: is God or is he himself its center? Will he declare himself to be autonomous and no longer a steward in the service of the Owner, though he is Lord of all?

In choosing against the Source of life Man plunged himself into death. The death that he found, however, was not the death of a corpse. The structure of relationships in which Man had been created continued, but deprived of the harmony, mutuality, joy, freedom, innocence, sense of responsibility and proportion that had characterized these relationships as they had been designed and put into effect by God. The true Center had been pushed aside, and an autonomous human center had taken his place. Alienation between God and Man, fragmentation in society, guilt in the soul, Man no longer the steward of a good creation—this was the new world that Man's folly brought into being. Millennia before they were written, the words of Yeats were true: "Things fall apart; the center cannot hold; mere anarchy is loosed upon the world . . . and everywhere the ceremony of innocence is drowned."

In this calamitous situation the mandate given in paradise remained unchanged: be fruitful and multiply, fill the earth, subdue it, have dominion. Amidst distortion, disruption, and universal disenchantment a basic continuity persisted, destined to endure until world's end. God did not give up the work to which he had put his hand: Man remained Man, *imago Dei,* and the world continued to reveal the *vestigia Dei.*

Deepening and diversification of the mandate began already in the first generation and has continued unabated in the history of Man. Early on diversification led to specialization, which in turn laid the foundation for the prodigious developments in the life and culture of Man. The first instance is the projected building of the tower of Babel "with its top in the heavens" (Gen. 11:4).

And throughout the history of civilization we see achievements of amazing ingenuity, refinement, and power in architecture, communication, science, art, social organization, and all other areas of human endeavor, culminating and possibly bankrupting in the universal obsession with technology.

In the historical manifestation of the four relationships in which the image of God is structured, the contrast between the lines of Cain and Seth is marked. The tenor of godlessness obtrudes in the former along with a distinct concern for the improvement of life in the face of an environment that has ceased to be wholly beneficent under God's displeasure with Man's sin. The line of Seth betrays no untoward acts and is marked by a tradition of piety. Among Cain and his descendants the direction of life is merely horizontal. But it does not appear that verticality was maintained in the line of Seth either. On the contrary, the two lines blended, and the Sethian tradition was wholly absorbed by the Cainitic: "The Lord saw that the wickedness of man was great in the earth, and that every imagination of the thoughts of his heart was only evil continually." Only Noah found favor in the eyes of God. He was a righteous man, blameless in his generation, for he walked with God (Gen. 6:5-9).

Although the line of Seth had expressed Man's true relationship to God, no family or social unit had come into being that found its particular calling or *raison d'être* in such a stewardship. Both in the state of innocence and in the state of sin God had dealt with mankind as a whole, as a unitary social entity. He had done so in three chronologically successive stages: in the stage of innocence, in the stage between the fall and the flood, and in the stage between the flood and the building of the tower of Babel. All three efforts to produce a godly human race had not only fallen short of the divine intention and expectation; they had been thoroughly and massively frustrated by disobedience in the Garden of Eden, by the degeneration that led to the flood, and by the pride that created the rebellion at Babel.

From that event on God pursued a radically different course. He chose one man, Abram, an Aramean Semite, who would be both an example of devout God-relatedness and the progenitor of a nation and people—Israel—in which the fear of God would be the hallmark of distinction. It is noteworthy that this Abrahamic line produced no great imperial power and little of the varied and richly developed artistic, political, literary, and philosophical attainment so characteristic of surrounding civilizations. Even though Israel was geographically in the very center of a succession of mighty imperial powers, the astounding achievements of Egypt, Babylon, Assyria, Persia, Greece, and Rome, and others of lesser but nevertheless worthy repute seem to have made little impression on the Jewish mind.

Yet all of these, Jews and Gentiles alike, were inseparably and indissolubly one in the creationally given heritage of the image of God, which was never destroyed and therefore never wholly lost. That is to say, they were one in the universal, unbreakable bond of common humanity.

From these considerations one is tempted to suggest that God in calling Abram had effected a division of labor among the nations. Israel would work out the implications of Man's relationship to God, and the other nations, the *goyim,* would develop the horizontally oriented aspects of Man as the *imago Dei.* Eventually the two streams would flow together again into the fullness of the ocean of humanity, with Jesus the Son of Man, the unblemished image of the Father, the mediator in history of the grand design. Each component in the divine-human relationship would make its own contribution to the reconciliation of Man with God and, in the process, of Man with Man. Is this perhaps the meaning of Pentecost?

Such a reading of history would ignore both the biblical and secular record of Man's religious history. The *goyim* were everywhere religiously active—so much so that their whole life from the peasant to the king turned around religious apprehensions. The king was intimately related to and at times identified with the national god. Temples, priesthood, sacrifice and celebration, soothsaying and worship were inseparable from people and state. In Assyria Shamash the sun-god and Sin the moon-god, in Babylonia Bel (also known as Marduk) the state-god, in Persia Ahura Mazda, in Palestine Baal and Moloch, and other major and lesser deities received the worship of their devotees. This religious life in turn inspired temple construction, constituted the source of the religious power of the priesthoods, and formed the basis of the whole ritual of sacrifice and worship. Archaeological discoveries of shrines, altars, sacred pillars, libation stands, and religious artifacts have been common. Religion was in no small degree the driving power of ancient civilizations.

But religion as a basic motif in the life of the nations is even more subject to deterioration than are life's activities on the horizontal plane. Indeed, the quality of the life of Man on all scores is determined by the quality of his relationship to God. It was for this reason that God chose one man, Abram, in whom and in whose posterity to exemplify, under the condition of sin, the true life of Man under God. But the exemplification of that life in a single people, even were it to be altogether successful, would not be the realization of the divine plan for Man's redemption. That plan envisaged blessing for "all the families of the earth" through that one man (Gen. 12:3b). It is therefore decisively critical to understand Abraham's relationship to that larger end, and this is dramatically symbolized in his willing subjection to the enigmatic figure of Melchizedek.

Let it be said first of all that Abram was not an Israelite, he was not a Jew, and his given name in his native land was not Abraham but Abram. Rather, in him the nation known as Israel and the people known as the Jews find their origin. He was one of the many nomadic people known as Arameans. Israel was taught to say, "A wandering Aramean was my father; and he went down into Egypt" (Deut. 26:5). As such he was given the great promises and *thereupon* was circumcised as a seal of the faith that he had exercised *as an Aramean.* In Romans 4:1-12 Paul makes this point importantly. The pagan character of the family Abram had left behind is shown by Rachel's theft of her father's household gods when she fled with Jacob to accompany him on his return to Canaan (Gen. 31:25-35). This is further attested in Joshua 24:2-3:

> And Joshua said to all the people, "Thus says the Lord, the God of Israel, 'Your fathers lived of old beyond the Euphrates, Terah, the father of Abraham and of Nahor; and they served other gods. Then I took your father Abraham from beyond the River . . . and made his offspring many.' "

There is thus no difference between the ethnic origins of Abraham's family and of the *goyim.* The religious differentiation between Israel and the *goyim* was wholly due to a divine intervention in the form of redemptive revelation given to Abraham and his posterity but not to the nations around them. Neither biblical nor extrabiblical data warrant the assumption of some sort of religious quality or superiority in Abraham or his family that led God to choose him rather than another for his redemptive purposes.

A correspondingly unusual figure whom we meet in intimate conjunction with Abraham is Melchizedek. It would be difficult to find a more intriguing and puzzling figure in the entire Bible. Our interest in him stems from the three verses (Gen. 14:18-20) describing him as "king of Salem" (later, Jerusalem) and "priest of God Most High." In him, the priestly office was associated with the kingly, as was often the case in the nations of that period. In Israel, too, kings performed priestly services: David (2 Sam. 6:17; 24:21, 25), Solomon (1 Kings 3:3-4, 15; 8:62-64), Jeroboam (1 Kings 12:32-33), Jehu (2 Kings 10:23-24). Such a one is prominently mentioned in Psalm 110:4 as a future king of Israel, whom the Lord had sworn to make "a priest for ever after the order of Melchizedek." In the New Testament book of Hebrews his priesthood is commented on in three chapters (5–7), with no fewer than seven occurrences of the expression "after the order of Melchizedek."

The formula "order of Melchizedek" does not occur in Genesis 14:18-20. Its meaning is not explained in the only other Old Testament mention of it in Psalm 110:4 or in the passages in

Hebrews, all of which are taken from Psalm 110. They are all concerned to set forth the superiority of the priesthood of Christ over that of Aaron, but the significance of the crucial word "order" is not made clear. It is variously rendered in English commentaries as manner, character, institution, succession, likeness, type, and nature, but no one can say precisely what it is in Melchizedek that is imaged in these words. Meanwhile, two plain and helpful allusions in the basic Melchizedek reference in Genesis 4 are not elaborated either in Psalm 110 or in Hebrews 5–7. These allusions are "priest of God Most High" and "maker of heaven and earth."

For our own purposes in this chapter we should begin by noting the factual background which is the context of Melchizedek's appearance in Genesis 14:18-20.

When Abraham with his band of trained warriors returned to the Sodom-Gomorrah area after defeating the raiding armies of Chedorlaomer and his allies, he was welcomed back by the king of Sodom and by Melchizedek, king of Salem, the latter bringing out bread and wine (Gen. 14:1-20). The point of chief significance here is that Melchizedek is identified as "priest of God Most High," who is the "maker of heaven and earth," and that he blessed Abraham and received tithes from him of the booty he had captured. Obviously, Melchizedek is presented here as a flesh-and-blood historical personage, a local king, not as some mysterious mythical figure who appears to take part in an occult ritual and then disappears.

The designation of Melchizedek as "priest of God Most High" is not a self-designation, nor is it cited as a report about him. It is made on the authority of the inspired writer himself. Its validity would seem to be borne out by Melchizedek's confession of "God Most High" as "maker of heaven and earth." In these words Abraham would recognize him as a spiritual brother who worshiped and served the same God that he acknowledged. Moments after receiving Melchizedek's blessing and giving his tithe, Abraham, in declining the offer of the king of Sodom to let him keep recaptured goods stolen from Sodom by Chedorlaomer, uses these words: "I have sworn to the Lord God Most High, maker of heaven and earth, that I would not take . . . anything that is yours" (14:22-23). Clearly, the same God who had called Abraham out of the *goyim* was confessed by Melchizedek.

In other words, there was evidence here of *worship* of God the Creator, and the king of Salem was either a priest or the high priest of the worshiping community. He represented a relationship to God that, had it been universally or even broadly accepted by fallen Man, would have averted the flood, forestalled the confusion of tongues at Babel, made unnecessary the calling and separation of Abraham, and brought Christ into the world without the long interval known to us as the history of Israel. Melchizedek represented the relationship of Man to God that was willed by God under the condition of sin, the relationship that Abel, Seth, Enoch, Noah, Shem, and, in all probability, Abram himself had sustained.

In the case of Melchizedek, however, the relationship was far more intense, symbolic, and foretelling. He was not only a priest, he was also a king. At that time the king was the nation, and his people were seen as in some very real sense "in" him. This is clear from the report in Genesis of the experience of his immediate contemporary, Abimelech, the king of Gerar in Philistia. When God rebuked Abimelech for having taken Sarah as his wife, he anxiously cast himself upon God for his people's sake: "Lord, wilt thou slay an innocent people?" This representative character God acknowledged: "If you do not restore her, know that you shall surely die, you, and all that are yours." Thereupon Abimelech chided Abraham, "What have you done to us? And how have I sinned against you, that you have brought on me and my kingdom a great sin?" (Gen. 20:1-9).

Melchizedek therefore incarnated, as it were, a people, a nation of the *goyim,* the humanity that was not-Israel. To serve that humanity Israel was being given its existence through Abraham, Israel's progenitor. Symbolically, the priest-king of Salem was universal Man and, as such, representative of "God Most High, maker of heaven and earth." In the historic meeting of Abraham and Melchizedek, the representative of provisional particularism gave tithes to and received blessing from the representative of God's permanent strategy of universal redemptive concern.

In the context of Melchizedek's royal priesthood in the service of God Most High, the Creator of heaven and earth, and of Abraham's primordial relationship to the chosen people, we should give full weight to the intimations of true faith apparent in this same geographic area in the extremely episodic Genesis account of Abraham's history. Note how the spiritual atmosphere differs between the two very similar stories of Abraham's sojourn in Egypt (Gen. 12:10-20) and in Gerar (Gen. 20:1-18). In both cases Abraham self-protectively introduced Sarah as his sister. Like Pharoah in Egypt, Abimelech took Sarah, but God came to him in a dream to warn: "Behold, you are a dead man, because of the woman whom you have taken; for she is a man's wife." Abimelech—who had not had sexual relations with Sarah—pleaded with God in wholly familiar terms, "Lord, wilt thou slay an innocent people? Did he not himself say to me, 'She is my sister'? And she herself said, 'He is my brother.' In the integrity of my heart and the innocence of my hands I have done this" (20:1-6). As Abraham admits when Abimelech confronts him, he had clearly misjudged the situation in Gerar: "I did it because I thought, There is no fear of God at all in this place" (20:11).

God also appeared to the Egyptian woman, Hagar, Sarah's maid, whom she had given to Abraham so that he might have a child by her. In the unhappiness which that arrangement brought, the angel of the Lord appeared to Hagar, and she acknowledged God's mercy to her: "Have I really seen God and remained alive after seeing him?" And she returned to Sarah and submitted to her (16:1-16).

When Abraham bargained with the Hittites for a burial place for Sarah, they were reluctant to sell it to him, wishing rather to give it outright, for, they said, "You are a prince of God among us" (23:6).

The line of faith from Adam to Abraham is tenuous but real. In the first generation after Adam, Abel brought a sacrificial offering that was pleasing to God (Gen. 4:4). In the days of Seth, still in the first generation, people began to call openly on God (4:26). Enoch "walked with God; and he was not, for God took him" (5:24). Noah was "a righteous man, blameless in his generation," and he walked with God (6:9); Shem and Japheth did not join Ham in dishonoring their father (9:20-23); Noah invoked blessing on Shem and increase on Japheth (9:26-27).

It would seem fair to assume that Abraham, Aramean in his descent and outlook, stood in this tradition. The words with which Genesis begins his story—"Now the Lord said to Abram, 'Go from your country and your kindred and your father's house to the land that I will show you. . . .' So Abram went, as the Lord had told him" (12:1, 4)—sound perfectly natural. There is no trace of doubt, uncertainty, or hesitation, even though the price of obedience was fully set forth: he must leave his homeland and family for a land that God would show him. This call comes in a social context in which "kindred" and "father's house" were everything. "So Abram went, as the Lord had told him." There seems implicit in this ready obedience an earlier knowledge of the God who had called him.

The fall, while instantaneous and catastrophic, nevertheless worked out its effects with gradual as well as immediate consequences. However profound the death of innocence, Adam did not die on the very day he ate of the forbidden fruit (Gen. 2:17). While opening the door to all manner of wickedness, the fall did not close it to the possibility of repentance and communion with God. Abel brought a sacrifice acceptable to God while Cain, not more under the guilt of sin than his brother, became his murderer (4:2-8). The possibility of communion with God became actuality in many cases, as we have seen, and there is no reason to believe that the concise account of many centuries in Genesis exhausts the number of those in early human history who led lives of devotion and humble obedience to God.

For later periods, Scripture presents impressive examples of faith at the fringes of Israel's life. Rahab the harlot had mercy on Israel's spies (Josh. 2), and in Hebrews 11:31 she is praised for her faith. Ruth the Moabitess would not leave her Israelite mother-in-law but went with her when she returned to Judah (Ruth 1:15-18) and, like Rahab, was taken up in the lineage of our Lord (Matt. 1:5). Hiram king of Tyre helped mightily in the building of the temple, and there are strong intimations that he was a believer (1 Kings 5:7; 2 Chron. 2:11-12). The queen of Sheba blessed the God of Israel (1 Kings 10:6-10).

Naaman, commander of the Syrian army, found healing in Israel and feared the God of Israel (2 Kings 5:15-19). (Especially noteworthy here is Elisha's tolerant "Go in peace" [vs. 19] in response to Naaman's compromise with principle where many today would draw a line.) In the first year of Cyrus king of Persia, the Lord stirred up his spirit to make a wonderful proclamation in response to God's speaking to him (Ezra 1:1-4).

Wise men from the East came to bring gifts to the Christ child (Matt. 2:1ff.). A Roman centurion in Capernaum had faith such as Jesus had not seen in Israel (Matt. 8:10ff.). To a Syro-Phoenician woman goes the honor of being the only person on record to best Jesus in a conversation, leading him to exclaim, "O woman, great is your faith! Be it done for you as you desire" (Matt. 15:21-28). In the house of a Roman centurion in Caesarea Peter learned that "in every nation any one who fears [God] and does what is right is acceptable to him" (Acts 10:35).

These passages emphasize, each in its own way, that during the centuries of Israel's particularism God had not surrendered the universal saving concern that characterized his relationship to Man from the fall to the calling of Abram. No matter how much Man was alienated from him, God continued to show that he regarded universal Man, humanity, as his never-rejected creature and companion. Again and again, by reason of some mysterious residuum within him or her or them, a person or a group of people here or there, in strange and unlooked-for situations, responded in faith to the call of God. Whether through hoary tradition or peripheral contact with Israel, God's call penetrated deep-rooted alienation to restore broken fellowship. By virtue of creation in the image of God, every human being is religious in the depth of his inner self. By reason of sin, Man pursues his destiny in a direction quite the opposite from that intended by the Creator. Fully retaining the *structure* of the image given in creation, he works at cross-purposes in all the *relations*—to God, to the neighbor, to self, and to the environing world—which constitute that structure. For all that, God never abandons love for his creation. Focusing on the *imago* of himself who stands at creation's head as vicegerent, God pursues him in his estrangement with the intent of reconciliation.

Of this intent, which is *divine* and therefore bears within itself inevitable realization, Melchizedek is the momentary but unforgettable representation. He is this, however, not in himself or by himself, but in his dramatic conjunction with Abraham. The coming together of Abraham and Melchizedek was more than a meeting of two leaders in which one acknowledged the other as the greater. It was a meeting of two dimensions of redemption—the particular and the universal, the passing and the abiding, the provisional means and the ultimate end. How clearly the principals understood this we cannot know. But some things we do know, and of these we must take note.

We know that the extraordinarily brief account of that meeting has survived all the vicissitudes through which the documents went that lie behind what we know as the Pentateuch or the Five Books of Moses.[1] It would not have been surprising if a perplexed editor somewhere down the centuries-long history of the formation of Genesis had simply dropped out this not obviously signif-

1. It is broadly agreed in Old Testament scholarly circles that the Pentateuch consists of a fusion of four major documents called the Jahwist, the Elohist, the Deuteronomic, and the Priestly. Great controversy and debate have attended the promulgation of this theory, the result of which is now best summarized in the words of H. H. Rowley: the documentary view "is only a working hypothesis which can be abandoned with alacrity when a more satisfying view is found, but cannot with profit be abandoned until then." See "Criticism" in the *International Standard Bible Encyclopedia,* fully revised ed., (Grand Rapids: Eerdmans, 1979), 1:817-21.

icant account. It was, however, retained. Some intuition of perhaps uncomprehended meaning prompted a caring solicitude.

Genesis 14 constitutes a problem for all serious students of the book. The commentaries make this plain with various linguistic, historical, and literary considerations. One of the best known, that of Gerhard von Rad, says that Genesis 14 "contains some of the most difficult and debated material in the patriarchal history, indeed in the entire historical part of the Old Testament."[2] Genesis as a whole is based on the Yahwist, Elohist, and Priestly documents, but Old Testament scholars are broadly agreed that chapter 14 does not fit into any of these characteristic sources. As a piece of literature Genesis 14 stands alone, an import from an unknown time and place. The author or redactor of Genesis found it meaningful to introduce it into the overall account of the Abraham story at this point.

Scholars of all hues agree with this, whatever their theological outlook. The Dutch commentator G. Ch. Aalders, certainly no admirer of the documentary theory of the history of the Pentateuch, judges that "we have here an old document, perhaps found in an archive here or there, which the biblical writer copied and inserted into his account."[3] With this conclusion Genesis scholars generally would seem to be in accord.[4]

The mystery attending the incorporation of chapter 14 into the Genesis record suggests that the compiler of the Abraham history or a subsequent editor found it meaningful to make it a part of the history. If this inference is correct, the question is: *what* is the factor that makes the inclusion of this chapter in the

2. Gerhard von Rad, *Genesis: A Commentary,* trans. John H. Marks (Louisville: Westminster Press, 1961), p. 170.

3. G. Ch. Aalders, *Het Boek Genesis,* 3 vols., in *Korte Verklaring der Heilige Schrift* (Kampen: J. H. Kok, 1936), 2:34.

4. The following other authorities may be mentioned: W. Brueggemann, *Genesis,* 1982; S. R. Driver, *The Book of Genesis,* 3rd edition, 1904; H. C. Leupold, *Exposition of Genesis,* Vol. I, 1956; J. Skinner, *Genesis,* in the series *International Commentary,* 1910; A. Van Selms, *Genesis,* Vol. I, 1967 (Dutch); G. Westerman, *Genesis, A Practical Commentary,* 1977.

Genesis account *meaningful?* In seeking to answer this, we shall focus on the three-verse Melchizedek story (vv. 18-20). This does not abstract these verses from the rest of the chapter, which obviously sets the context for the meeting of Melchizedek and Abraham. We confine ourselves to verses 18-20 as the climax of the account of Abraham's defeat of Chedorlaomer and his allies.

Commentators' explanations of the significance of Genesis 14, though reasonable, are far from unanimous. One sees Melchizedek, having a faith akin to Abraham's, as the forerunner of David and David's house. If even Abraham, the father of Israel, gave him tithes, how much more should the people of Israel recognize and yield to the royal authority of David.

Another interpretation sees Salem, in which Melchizedek was priest, as the forerunner of the later Jerusalem, and thus having a priesthood that foreshadowed the later Zadokite priesthood in the temple in Jerusalem. This follows from the fact that Melchizedek worshiped the same God that Abraham worshiped.

In still another, Hebrews 5–7 views Melchizedek, because of his mysterious one-time appearance on the stage of history, as a sort of timeless eternity figure, whose priesthood can thus be seen as foretelling the eternal priesthood of Christ.

But none of these interpretations relates its understanding of the Melchizedek-Abraham meeting to the experience of the original narrator of the story. What thoughts must have occupied the mind of the first chronicler of that great and fateful drama! He had faithfully recorded the tradition of Man's history from the Garden of Eden to the time of Abraham. This was a history not simply of two primal parents and their offspring. It was a history of the unitary entity mankind, the human race, which the writer of Genesis 1 called the image and likeness of God. Those constituting that race would be stewards of all things given into their care. In the name and in the service of the Creator they would govern the world and all things in it. But all this had come to naught. Instead of recording a history of joyful obedience, development, and growth, the chronicler had been compelled to report the fall from integrity into the bondage of sin and death.

He had also recorded the faithfulness of the Creator, who had not forsaken the work of his hands but had set about to redeem the race from its sin. But this effort, far from effecting redemption, had ended in judgment, first in the catastrophe of the flood, then in the dispersion of the race from its center at Babel. Mankind had proven to be intractable, ungovernable, wholly set on its autonomous intent.

At some point following the debacle at Babel, God had undertaken a third effort at redemption. This, too, the writer had learned through the oral tradition. But in reporting it, he described a radical shift in the divine strategy. The story carried by the continuing tradition changed from describing redemptive relations between God and mankind *as a whole* to recording a redemptive relationship between God and the *one man Abram* and his family.

This also the writer had committed to documentary form. His report began thus:

> Now the Lord said to Abram,
> "Go from your country and your kindred and your father's house to the land that I will show you. And I will make of you a great nation, and I will bless you, and make your name great, so that you will be a blessing. I will bless those who bless you, and him who curses you I will curse; and by you all the families of the earth shall be blessed." (Gen. 12:1-3)

Here was much for the keen mind of the chronicler to ponder. Consider in terms of ethnic psychology alone how great his puzzlement must have been. Abram must leave his native land, its fields and forests and rivers and mountains, its people, its language, its customs, and its history. In so doing, he must leave his relations, the rich society of the extended family. And then came the climactic, crushing demand: "and your father's house." Leave your closest kin, take only your wife and your nephew Lot, your household servants and your movable goods. Surrender it all to an irrecoverable past and go. Just go. Go where? Where God shows you.

Such were the sacrifices demanded of Abram. But there were compensating promises. He would become a great nation. God would bless him and make his name great, and he would be a blessing to others. Moreover, his obedience would bring enrichment to those who would help him, and it would put a curse on those who opposed him. And in the end, he would be a blessing to "all the families of the earth." He would become a man of universal significance, a boon to the whole society of Man. Abram, standing between all that he knew himself concretely to have and all that had been promised to him by God, did not calculate. He took God at his word and "went, as the Lord had told him" (Gen. 12:4). The Lord led him to Canaan, then to Egypt, then back again to Canaan. There the Lord said to him, "All the land which you see I will give to you and to your descendants for ever. . . . Arise, walk through the length and the breadth of the land, for I will give it to you . . . ," and there he built an altar to the Lord (Gen. 13:15-18).

From the writer's viewpoint, the providence of God up to this point must have seemed ambiguous, if not obscure. The revelation he had been given to record had had one dominant theme: whether in the state of integrity before the fall or in the state of sin after the fall, God deals with his *imago* as a solidarity, as a whole, as a unitary organism. But now Providence seemed to forsake this principle. The calling of Abram to become the father of a separate people would inevitably bring into being those who would *not* be God's people, that is, the *goyim.* How must he understand this?

There was, of course, an important qualification of such reflections in the very heart of Abram's call: the promise that in him "all the families of the earth" would be blessed. But this unexplicated future involvement in the well-being of the human family worldwide seemed to comport ill with the present call to separation. It could only deepen the perplexity created by the sudden change in time-honored course.

It was presumably at this juncture that the document we know as Genesis 14 came to the attention of the writer or of a later editor. (Conceivably, the original writer did not labor under the problem we have attributed to him. He may not have been all that theologically inclined. Perhaps he was just a very competent chronicler of events. It makes perfectly good sequential sense to skip from the last verse of Genesis 13 to the first verse of chapter 15.) What is certain is that, in the providence guiding the history of the composition of the book of Genesis, *somebody* was given the discernment to see the significance of the X document and to make it part of the manuscript he was writing or the existing account he was editing. Somebody saw the abrupt change in the pattern of divine concern for the salvation of mankind as a whole signaled by the calling of Abram.

We have spoken broadly of the meaning of this change. Let us now become specific. Basically, the calling of Abram to become the father of a separate nation did not signify an abandonment of the nations to their own devices, but rather the initiation of a new strategy to call them back to God. The universalism of God's redemptive concern for mankind, characteristic of the fall-to-flood and the flood-to-Babel eras, was replaced by the particularism of God's redemptive relationship to Israel. When that relationship should have served its purpose, the redemption and the redemptive power so revealed would be deployed to embrace again the whole of mankind, with a view to the restoration of the *imago Dei* to its original scope and integrity.

Pentecost was the great turning point that ended the strategy of Abrahamic, or Jewish, particularism and renewed the primal policy of universalism. As mankind fell apart at Babel due to the confusion of language attendant upon its sin, so people from all the nations of the world were representatively reunited at Pentecost through the spiritual language of the gospel into a new fellowship known as the church.

The significance of the Melchizedek story is eloquent in foreshadowing this history. What figure in the history of the Old Testament or in the church of the New, apart from Jesus, is greater than Abraham, the chosen by God, the progenitor of the Jewish people, the father of believers? There is none. Neither Moses, nor David, nor any of the prophets, nor John the Baptist, nor Paul, nor any other apostle is greater than Abraham in the family of God on earth or in the kingdom of heaven. Yet this great man bowed to Melchizedek, received blessing from him, and gave to him a tenth of the spoils gained on the battlefield. In all this, Abraham did not speak, did not act other than to present a tithe to the representative of the greater redemptive dimension.

The writer or editor, finding a document that told this story (now Genesis 14) standing alongside of rather than within the tradition, sensed here the resolution of his perplexity. He could see Melchizedek as a symbol, a type of the humanity that was for a time left to walk in its own way but, as a constant neighbor of Abraham's offspring, would be awaiting, if unconsciously, the day of its adoption into the family of God.

The separation of Abraham from the nations was not a final separation. It was not a substitute for the full reclamation of all the nations and peoples of the world. It was a strategic withdrawal to effect a centuries-long preparation for the coming of the great High Priest, whom Melchizedek foreshadowed, on behalf of the humanity in whose service God had called Abram to become Abraham.

In the execution of this strategy there was, though long obscured to the human eye, a hidden purpose at work which gave an undreamed-of meaning to the promised "great nation" that Abram was to become. A "great nation" in Abraham's time was pretty much what it is today: self-centered, proud, threatening to powerful neighbors, exploitative of weaker neighbors, always exulting in its many-sided might. Such were the nations Melchizedek represented, devout and gentle though he may have been. We see Abram here in the form of a servant. The father of God's dispensation of particularism acknowledges the universal *goyim* as greater than himself and himself as the servant of all. Whatever understanding Abram had of Melchizedek's seniority, it was necessarily limited, something he saw "through a glass darkly." And this holds as well for the writer of the account or its subsequent editor.

This does not, however, remove those elements of Abraham's experience that are solidly known: that he had a call from God to be set apart for a special purpose, that he obeyed the call in spite of intimidating odds, that he knew himself to have been given a place of universal significance in God's plan, that he had been blessed by Melchizedek in the name of the very God whom he himself served, and that he had given a tithe to this royal person even though he had just come victorious out of the battle that had occasioned the blessing.

These considerations are made the more important by the circumstance that Melchizedek appears only once on the screen of history. It surrounds the entire drama with an aura of symbolism which we from our post-Pentecostal vantage point should not ignore in evaluating its meaning. Abraham belonged to that phase in the history of redemption in which

> the prophets who prophesied of the grace that was to be yours searched and inquired about this salvation; they inquired what person or time was indicated by the Spirit of Christ within them when predicting the sufferings of Christ and the subsequent glory. It was revealed to them that they were serving not themselves but you, in the things which have now been announced to you by those who preached the good news to you through the Holy Spirit sent from heaven, things into which angels long to look. (1 Pet. 1:10-12)

Together with the angelic host we can now see that God the Creator of heaven and earth seeks in Christ the restoration to integrity of the *imago Dei* that was defiled. He created the entity called mankind, and he redeems the entity called mankind. What he made in the joy of creation, what was lost in the tragedy of the fall, he reclaims through the blood of the cross. It means the return to integrity of God's *alter ego,* the restoration in grace-enhanced beauty of the full *imago Dei*, which Abraham somehow discerned in the person of Melchizedek, "priest of God Most High" and a forerunner of "all the families of the earth."

Chapter III

The Misnomer "Total Depravity"

Behold, this alone I found, that God made man upright, but they have sought out many devices.

Ecclesiastes 7:29

All Christian theology must come to terms with two magnitudes in the human situation. They are commonly known as *sin* and *grace.* Sin is Man's revolt against the will of God for his life. Grace, in the sense of forfeited divine favor, is God's response in dealing with revolting Man. Philosophy deals with two analogous dimensions known as *good* and *evil.* The theological categories of sin and grace focus specifically on Man. They are mentioned in that order because they arose in that temporal sequence. Without sin in the life of Man there would be no need of grace from the side of God. In philosophy good and evil are mentioned in that order because they are seen respectively as positive and negative values, without reference to the order of their appearance.

This order of dealing with the categories in question is worth noting because of the fundamentally different bases underlying theological and philosophical treatment of them. The basis for the theological discussion of sin and grace is divine revelation.

The philosophical discussion of good and evil arises out of the effort of the human mind to understand the nature of these two dimensions as observed in all, but especially human, existence.

Of course, the theologian and the philosopher do not live in hermetically sealed compartments. There are philosophers who confess the name of Christ, and there are theologians with philosophical interests. Certainly no theologian can ignore the correspondence between the "sin" and "grace" found in Scripture and the "good" and "evil" found in life. Nevertheless, theologians derive their primary categories of comprehension from revelation and philosophers derive them from reflection on observation and experience (which in the case of the Christian philosopher will include a faith commitment).

Our present discussion here is a frankly theological one, specifically in its interest in viewing Man as image of God. The reference to philosophy is appropriate because it underscores that the theological problem faced in this book is not the general and more abstract problem of good and evil, but the concrete situation of Man as image of God *under the conditions of sin and grace.*

In no area of Reformed theology is the doctrine of the image of God so significant as in the department of systematic theology known as Anthropology, the doctrine of Man. In this chapter we seek to assess the effect of the fall of Man into sin on the image as it came whole and pure from the hand of God. In so doing, we confront the fact that Reformed theology accepts as nonnegotiable two irreconcilable concepts: the retention, however marred, of the image of God after the fall, and the total depravity of Man. The contrast lies not between Man's sinfulness and his being image of God, but between his *total depravity* and his being image of God. In human and Christian experience, sinfulness in essential being and in concrete words and deeds does not exclude the active presence of *good* in life. This can hardly be said of depravity, particularly not when it is total and constitutes, *as* total depravity, the central being of Man in relation to God under the condition of sin.

In seeking to speak and write in a way that faithfully reflects not only God's revelation but also his own deepest intentions, the theologian should not use words and expressions which, while understood (or perhaps excused) in a given circle of believers, cause needless offense in the world outside the church and even in the vast family of God that has received its Christian life through the channel of other traditions. When theological language becomes jargon, a disservice is done to the gospel.

The pertinence of this comment to the Reformed community is evident from the fact that its discussion of the doctrine of total depravity has usually begun with stating what the term does *not* mean. A notable instance is Louis Berkhof's widely used *Reformed Dogmatics,* which introduces the subject with these words: "This phrase is often misunderstood, and therefore calls for careful discrimination. Negatively, it does not imply. . . ." Then follow (a), (b), (c), and (d), informing the reader what is excluded from the concept.[1] The exclusions limit the depravedness of the alleged depravity but by no means take out of the term what the entire English-speaking world—from the *Oxford English Dictionary* to the reasonably literate man on the street—understands by it.

When one in good faith tells a person who does not know Christ that he is sinful or that he is a sinner, he may be embarrassed but will not deny it. For most people, the word "sin" does not have the vertical reference that it has for the Christian, but is an accepted designation for moral evil. On the other hand, to tell someone that he is totally depraved will certainly offend and possibly outrage him, because it means *only* moral baseness, moral turpitude, which the secular as well as the Christian world denounces.

In Christian witness the words "sin," "sinner," "sinfulness" can form a point of contact to introduce a God-ward dimension into the discussion. In no way will this happen with the word "depravity." The imputation of the moral dimension that this

1. Louis Berkhof, *Reformed Dogmatics* (Grand Rapids: Eerdmans, 1932), 1:234.

word occasions will raise a barrier of indignation which adducing Berkhof's four exclusions will do little to allay. The milder words of Ecclesiastes 7:29—"Behold, this alone I found, that God made man upright, but they have sought out many devices"—make possible a full exposition of the biblical teaching on sin without resorting to self-defeating language.

In the present context, however, we are only marginally interested in the advisability of using the word "depravity" in preaching, writing, and Christian witness. Our concern is with the legitimacy of a basic Reformed theological principle. In considering this problem we may safely take John Calvin's *Institutes of the Christian Religion* as basis for discussion.[2] Calvin is the undisputed father of Reformed theology, and in Book II of his classic work he discusses all aspects of the doctrine as it bears on the image of God concept. Since Calvin's doctrine of total depravity continues to be held in much of Reformed credal and, to an extent, in academic theology, it is important to understand and evaluate it theologically. We shall do so first in terms of Calvin's use of moral categories, and second in terms of his understanding of the *imago Dei* concept.

Calvin sees what Man is in the light of the Person that God is, and therefore in the light of the absolute perfection of righteousness, wisdom, and power that characterize his nature. When we measure ourselves by that standard, then "what wonderfully impressed us under the name of wisdom will stink in its very foolishness. What wore the face of power will prove itself the most miserable weakness" (I.i.2). This theme is developed in the first five chapters of Book II:

> For our nature is not only destitute and empty of good, but so fertile and fruitful of every evil that it cannot be idle . . . that whatever

2. All quotations from the *Institutes* are from the translation of Ford Lewis Battles in *The Library of Christian Classics,* Volumes XX and XXI, ed. John T. McNeill (Philadelphia: Westminster Press, 1960). The references are to Book, Chapter, and Section and are included in the text.

> is in man, from the understanding to the will, from the soul even to the flesh, has been defiled and crammed with this concupiscence. Or, to put it more briefly, the whole man is of himself nothing but concupiscence. (II.i.8)

> . . . the whole man is overwhelmed—as by a deluge—from head to foot, so that no part is immune from sin, and all that proceeds from him is to be imputed to sin. (II.i.9)

> . . . in man's perverted and degenerate nature some sparks still gleam. These show him to be a rational being, differing from brute beasts, because he is endowed with understanding. Yet, secondly, they show this light choked with dense ignorance, so that it cannot come forth effectively.
>
> Similarly the will, because it is inseparable from man's nature, did not perish, but was so bound to wicked desires that it cannot strive after the right. (II.ii.12)

These declarations, and the whole argument of which they are a part, are succinctly summarized in the last sentence of the last paragraph of these chapters in grim and unsparing words:

> Therefore let us hold this as an undoubted truth which no siege engines can shake: the mind of man has been so completely estranged from God's righteousness that it conceives, desires, and undertakes, only that which is impious, perverted, foul, impure, and infamous. The heart is so steeped in the poison of sin, that it can breathe out nothing but a loathsome stench. But if some men occasionally make a show of good, their minds nevertheless ever remain enveloped in hypocrisy and deceitful craft, and their hearts bound by inner perversity. (II.v.19)

These quotations may leave the impression that Calvin was blind to the commonly observed manifestations of excellence and virtue in the unregenerate. On the contrary, he frankly acknowledges their gifts:

> Shall we say that the philosophers were blind in their fine observation and artful description of nature? . . . Shall we say that they are insane who developed medicine, devoting their labor to our

> benefit? What shall we say of all the mathematical sciences? . . . No, we cannot read the writings of the ancients on these subjects without great admiration. (II.ii.15)

But this is not a commendation of men, but a recognition of the gifts of God evident in them:

> If we regard the Spirit of God as the sole fountain of truth, we shall neither reject the truth itself, nor despise it wherever it shall appear, unless we wish to dishonor the Spirit of God. . . . Those men whom Scripture [1 Cor. 2:14] calls "natural men" were, indeed, sharp and penetrating in their investigation of inferior things. Let us, accordingly, learn . . . how many gifts the Lord left to human nature even after it was despoiled of its true good. (II.ii.15)

So far as the unregenerate themselves are concerned,

> . . . however admirable they may be regarded on account of their reputation for virtue, [they] not only deserve no reward but rather punishment, because by the pollution of their hearts they defile God's good works. For even though they are God's instruments for the preservation of human society . . . yet they carry out these good works of God very badly. For they are restrained from evil-doing not by genuine zeal for good but either by mere ambition or by self-love, or some other perverse motive. (III.xiv.3)
>
> We therefore hold to be beyond doubt what ought to be a mere commonplace even to one indifferently versed in the Scriptures, that in men not yet truly sanctified works manifesting even the highest splendor are so far away from righteousness before the Lord that they are reckoned sins. (III.xiv.8)

In rendering so austere and unbending a judgment on those standing outside the circle of God's redeeming grace, Calvin considers that he is wholly within the context and spirit of Scripture. From the vast fund of biblical passages that on first sight appear to lend solid support to his theological judgment, we may note the following which are among the ones he quotes in Book II, chapters 1 to 5: Genesis 6:5 (the wickedness of Man was great in the earth and his imagination only evil continually),

Genesis 8:21 (the imagination of Man's heart is evil from youth), Psalm 94:11 (the Lord knows the thoughts of Man to be but a breath), Jeremiah 17:5 (cursed is the man who makes flesh his arm), Matthew 15:13 (every plant which the Father has not planted will be rooted up), John 3:6 (that which is born of the flesh is flesh), John 6:44 (no one can come to Jesus unless the Father who sent Jesus draws him), John 15:5 (a branch cannot bear fruit unless it abides in Christ the vine), Romans 3:10-18 (none is righteous, none seeks for God, mouths are full of curses, feet are swift to shed blood, there is no fear of God before their eyes), Romans 8:7 (the mind set on the flesh is hostile to God; it does not and cannot submit to God's law), 1 Corinthians 1:20 (has not God made foolish the wisdom of the world?), 1 Corinthians 2:14 (the unspiritual man does not receive the gifts of the Spirit of God, for they are folly to him), 2 Corinthians 3:5 (we are not competent of ourselves; our competence is from God), Ephesians 4:17-19 (Gentiles live in the futility of their minds, given up to licentiousness), 2 Thessalonians 2:11-12 (God sends a strong delusion on those about to perish to make them believe what is false).

Impressive and relevant though this compilation may seem, a second look reveals that Calvin's stringent interpretation of these and similar passages is open to very serious strictures. These may be discussed under two major headings—his use of Scripture and his understanding of the image of God.

There is no doubt that a major reason for Calvin's authoritative position as a systematic theologian is his versatile use of Scripture. His amazing absorption and appropriation of biblical data enable him to bring to bear in his argument passages which it would not occur to a less astute student of the Bible to adduce. But this virtue is by no means uniform in Calvin, and in his effort to establish the doctrine of total depravity his record is far from impressive. At one point he makes use of Paul's collection (Romans 3:10-18) of passages from six different psalms plus one passage from Isaiah to establish the depravity of mankind. By means of the customary "it is written," Calvin presents them as a single piece of writing, even altering pronouns to suit his purpose. To do this in a pastoral letter in apostolic times is one thing; to do it in a work of systematic theology fifteen centuries later is quite another. Indeed, Calvin appears to have been aware of this. Introducing his discussion of the passage he says,

> I shall not toil in proving the applicability of these passages, in order that they may not seem to have been inappropriately seized upon by the apostle. I shall proceed as if these statements had first been made by Paul, not drawn from the Prophets. (II.iii.2)

Presumably Calvin judged that Paul as an instrument of God's infallible inspiration had the authority to bring together these several quite distinct passages into one massive validation of his teaching concerning the sinful character of unregenerate Man. But what could be accepted in Paul's time and possibly excused in Calvin's is no longer either acceptable or excusable. In the course of the centuries the Holy Spirit has fulfilled his promise to lead God's people into the truth (John 16:13), not only as to the meaning of Scripture but also as to the way it should be read. The critical study of the Bible has been and continues to be a valid means of deepening the understanding of Scripture, also in evangelical circles, ever since James Orr as general editor of the *International Standard Bible Encyclopedia* (1913) published in it his decisive article on biblical criticism. The sin of many evangelicals has been that in their extensive use of the *ISBE* they ignored to their own great loss in credibility and effectiveness the basic principles laid down by Orr in his contribution.

At this point I call attention only to the fundamental consideration of reading the Bible *contextually.* It would be obviously improper to read the text "There is therefore now no condemnation for those who are in Christ Jesus" (Rom. 8:1) as saying, "There is therefore now no condemnation." Similarly, the passages Paul cites stand in contexts that do not allow Calvin to establish from them the total depravity of mankind. In Psalms 14 and 53 there is a clear distinction between "all the evildoers" and "the ungodly" on the one hand and "the generation of the righteous" and "the poor" on the other. In Psalm 140, those who "make their tongue sharp as a serpent's" are distinguished from "the afflicted" and "the needy," to whom Paul's "their tongue" does not apply. In Psalm 10:7 it is not the poor, the innocent, the hapless, the meek, the fatherless, and the oppressed whose mouth is filled with cursing, deceit, and oppression. Isaiah 59:7 distinguishes those whose "feet run to evil" from "innocent blood," and in Psalm 36:1 he who has "no fear of God before his eyes" is quite other than "the children of men [who] take refuge in the shadow of thy wings" (v. 7). Calvin could, of course, reply that "my people" and similar references to members of the household of faith refer to believers, who have had the curse removed from them. But that still leaves the poor, the afflicted and needy, the hapless, the meek, the fatherless, the innocent, and the oppressed, who do not necessarily become believers because of their disadvantaged position.

For Calvin, the absolute, ineradicable, and eternal distinction between elect and reprobate is a practical working hypothesis in the ongoing present of history-in-process. He would no doubt agree that it is impossible to separate out the two here and now. But he is very sure that the alleged good which the reprobate perform is, in the eyes of the all-knowing God, only corrupt, rotten, concupiscent. They are incapable of harboring a motive for their "goodness" that is acceptable to God.

> Therefore, because they do not look to the goal that God's wisdom prescribes, what they do, though it seems good in the doing, yet by its perverse intention is sin. . . . Therefore, true righteousness was not in them, because duties are weighed not by deeds but by ends. (III.xiv.3)

In the Bible, however, the deed plays a powerful role, and its motivation often does not come into consideration or, if it does, is evaluated in terms of existing standards of propriety or worth. The parable of "the good Samaritan" presents an example of love in action on the part of one whom all Jesus' hearers must have regarded as not being a child of God's covenant and therefore not one with God's people. The "rich young ruler" could not bring himself to give to the poor all that he had, but when he testified that he had observed from his youth all the demands of the second table of the law, "Jesus looking upon him loved him" (Mark 10:17-22). In the parable of the forgiven but not forgiving servant (Matt. 18:23-35), the motives of the king and the fellow servants are not stated, but their actions are sufficient to constitute an example both of God's justice and of his clemency.

Most of the book of Proverbs consists of homely sayings, many drawn from sources external to Israel, about whose value all can agree. The "wise man" is one who conducts himself in accordance with them. Nowhere does the book mention or even hint that only a God-fearing Israelite can do so sincerely and in a manner pleasing to God. The moral exhortations of the prophets of the Old Testament and of the apostles in the New make plain that mere external observance of the precepts of the law will not excuse those whose hearts are not right with God. But they do not say that the praiseworthy deeds and attitudes of the generality of persons who are not God-fearing are the fruit of only hypocrisy and inward rottenness. Even where the rottenness is plain in the life of God's own people, he does not take their rejection of him as the last word. For ten chapters Hosea alternately thunders against and pleads with sinful Israel. At last mercy wins out over threat and judgment. He exclaims on God's behalf, "How can I give you up, O Ephraim! How can I hand you over, O Israel! . . . My heart recoils within me, my compassion grows warm and tender . . . ; for I am God and not man, the Holy One in your midst, and I will not come to destroy" (Hos. 11:8-9).

Calvin's discussion of Man's sinfulness and loss in the fall that cast him into ruin lacks such an identification with and hope for Man. There is no commerce between the two camps of the chosen and the rejected. The objective, analytical theologian reporting the eternal counsel of God cannot introduce into it the dimensions of either human hope or divine love for the unfavored segment of the human race, which is the object of God's wrath. For them the remains of the image of God are only and exclusively structural. As structured entity, the image exists; as living, breathing *personality* the image functions only by a perverse will to camouflage selfishness, ambition, envy, and hate in spite of all its admirable excellencies.

Systematic theology is not truly systematic when it structures the message of Scripture without including the whole range of divine emotions and not just concepts that arise out of considerations of intellect and will. The theologian dealing with the temporal history and eternal destiny of men must hear God's gentle rebuke to Jonah in his zeal for justice: "And should not I pity Nineveh, that great city, in which there are more than a hundred and twenty thousand persons who do not know their right hand from their left, and also much cattle?" (4:11).

The second standard for evaluating Calvin's doctrine of total depravity is his own theology of the image of God under the condition of sin. It consists basically of *surviving remnants* of the perfection that *once was* but is no more. The following passages may be noted:

> There is no doubt that Adam, when he fell from his state, was by this defection alienated from God. Therefore, even though we grant that God's image was not totally annihilated and destroyed in him, yet it was so corrupted that whatever remains is frightful deformity. (I.xv.4)

> Now God's image is the perfect excellence of human nature which shone in Adam before his defection, but was subsequently so vitiated and almost blotted out that nothing remains after the ruin except what is confused, mutilated, and disease-ridden. (I.xv.4)

> Let us, accordingly, learn [from the example of secular writers] how many gifts the Lord left to human nature even after it was despoiled of its true good. (II.ii.15)

> As the free gifts were withdrawn from man after the Fall, so the natural ones remaining were corrupted. . . . Not that the gifts could

> become defiled by themselves, seeing that they came from God. But to defiled man these gifts were no longer pure. (II.ii.16)

> We see in this diversity [of gifts] some remaining traces of the image of God, which distinguish the entire human race from the other creatures. (II.ii.17)

All these quotations show that Calvin allows only minimal value to the deposit of truth left to Man. Moreover, the traces and remains of the image left to mankind themselves constitute a "frightful deformity." They are "confused, mutilated, and disease-ridden." Granted that the gifts which God bestowed on Man at creation have been affected by human sin, yet it is hardly consonant with Calvin's own estimate of these remains to call them "misshapen ruins" (II.ii.12). His praise for the wisdom of ancient science does not allow such a denigration of the good gifts of God, which he says we may not esteem lightly "unless we wish to dishonor the Spirit of God" (II.ii.15). A gift of God is always good (cf. II.ii.16).

If the remains of the *imago Dei* in Man are truly that, they must be remains of the divine excellence in which Man was created. They may be very weak manifestations of the integral image, but as true sparks of a once brightly burning flame they are like faintly glowing coals, not hardened and dead cinders. What Calvin calls "sparks" (II.ii.12) must have, in however diminished a manner, the quality of fire. It would thus seem impermissible to say that the perversion of the image of God by sinful Man has so affected the life of Man that he can now truthfully be said to be "totally depraved."

In his painstaking study *Calvin's Doctrine of Man,* T. F. Torrance notes this inconsistency in Calvin's position. "It is difficult," he says, "to see how there can be any ultimate reconciliation between Calvin's doctrine of total perversity and his doctrine of a remnant of the *imago dei.*" But, Torrance adds, the fact that Calvin "can give them both in the same breath seems to indicate that he had no difficulty in reconciling them." He then continues,

> That there is an ultimate inconsistency seems demanded by Calvin's denial that there is any *seed of election* or any *germ of righteousness* in fallen man. In other words, both the doctrine of election as Calvin holds it and the doctrine of justification by faith alone seem to imply that there is *no remnant of the imago dei.*[3]

Calvin was not unaware of this weakness in his argument. He therefore sought a way to keep his exposition intact. A distinction must be made to the effect that

> there is one kind of understanding of earthly things; another of heavenly. I call "earthly things" those which do not pertain to God or his Kingdom . . . but which have their significance and relationship with regard to the present life and are, in a sense, confined within its bounds. I call "heavenly things" the pure knowledge of God, the nature of true righteousness, and the mysteries of the Heavenly Kingdom. (II.ii.13)

"Earthly things"—we might call them natural realities—include "government, household management, all mechanical skills, and the liberal arts." "Heavenly things"—spiritual realities—include "the knowledge of God and of his will, and the rule by which we conform our lives to it." In Calvin's treatment of the former (II.ii.13-17), we find his expressions of high praise for human skills. Sections 18 to the end of the chapter deal with the heavenly things. With respect to them, says Calvin, "the greatest geniuses are blinder than moles!" (II.ii.18). He understands John 1:4-5 to show "that man's soul is so illumined by the brightness of God's light as never to be without some slight flame or at least a spark of it; but that even with this illumination it does not comprehend God" (II.ii.19).

What Calvin is saying here is that the fall effected not only a catastrophic weakening of the *imago* but also a drastic loss in its essential content. The earthly things remain present in the form of a spark or a remnant, and even that is despoiled; the

3. T. F. Torrance, *Calvin's Doctrine of Man*, new ed. (Grand Rapids: Eerdmans, 1957), p. 93.

heavenly things are lost altogether. They have been "withdrawn" and are "extinguished." The Scholastic theologians had learned that from Augustine; and this teaching pleased Calvin:

> that the natural gifts were corrupted in man through sin, but that his supernatural gifts were stripped from him. For by the latter clause they understand the light of faith as well as righteousness. . . . From this it follows that he is so banished from the Kingdom of God that all qualities belonging to the blessed life of the soul have been extinguished in him, until he recovers them through the grace of regeneration. Among these are faith, love of God, charity toward neighbor, zeal for holiness and for righteousness.

The heavenly gifts are "adventitious" and for that reason "beyond nature" (II.ii.12). Torrance quite properly points out that "in this doctrine of the *imago dei,* Calvin agrees with the Roman Catholic view that the image of God must be related to a *supernatural gift.*"[4] Torrance is alluding here to that distinctive Roman Catholic doctrine of the *donum superadditum*, the "added gift." In Catholic theology this gift *is* the *imago Dei.* When Man was created he was created wholly human, but without the *imago*. This gift was *added* to his human nature to enable him to *earn* through obedience the bliss of eternal life. Adam's disobedience deprived him of the *imago* but left his humanity in its integrity. Without it, however, Man was more vulnerable to the weaknesses of his passions, which in due time did indeed prevail. For Calvin the whole of the *imago Dei* belonged to Adam in his integrity; after the fall he retained the natural or earthly part of it in the form of a remnant, but he was altogether deprived of the spiritual or heavenly aspect of the *imago.*

In Roman Catholic theology, therefore, Adam lost the image altogether in the fall, but retained his humanity fully. In Calvin's theology the earthly reference of the *imago* was a true part of Adam's "natural" earthbound life. Therefore he retained it after the fall. The spiritual part of the *imago,* however, was "adventi-

4. Torrance, *Calvin's Doctrine of Man,* p. 68.

tious," a supplementary entity that he could no longer use after the fall. For Calvin the fall created a division in the image of God—of which Man retained by far the lesser part. But even this remnant enabled him to attain to "no small dignity."

Calvin's theology of the *imago Dei* therefore raises the question whether there is any meaningful sense in which Man under the condition of sin can still be called "image of God." Several considerations call for attention here. Calvin writes:

> I now consider it sufficiently proved that whatever has to do with spiritual and eternal life is included under "image." . . . John confirms this same point in other words, declaring that "the life" which was from the beginning in God's Eternal Word "was the light of men" [John 1:4]. (I.xv.4)

It was John's intention to show "how man was created in God's image. Now God's image is the perfect excellence of human nature which shone in Adam before his defection" (I.xv.4). Clearly, the "life" and "light of men" is here just another designation of the "heavenly things."

Strangely, in II.ii.12, Calvin applies the very next verse of John 1—"The light still shines in the darkness, but the darkness comprehends it not"—to the merely "earthly things." These words, he says, show that

> first, in man's perverted and degenerate nature some sparks still gleam. These show him to be a rational being, differing from brute beasts, because he is endowed with understanding. Yet, secondly, they show this light choked with dense ignorance, so that it cannot come forth effectively. (II.ii.12)

The writer of the Gospel of John did not divide his text into verses. There is thus not the slightest ground for distinguishing between the "life" and the "light" of verse 4 and the "light" of verse 5. They refer to one and the same light and life—the light and life of the Eternal Word that became incarnate in Christ. Of this whole undivided Word, and with *special reference* to the earthly or "natural" aspect of his being, "some sparks still gleam" in the "perverted and degenerate nature" of Man. Calvin could not possibly discuss the image of God without referring to this classic text. But his unyielding adherence to the doctrine of total depravity, with its consequent bifurcation in the *imago Dei,* made a corresponding radical adjustment in the interpretation of the biblical *locus classicus* inevitable.

A word is in order here from the Dutch theologian Herman Bavinck, whose magisterial four-volume *Gereformeerde Dogmatiek* still speaks with authority on many great issues of the faith eighty years after its appearance. In an extensive discussion of the *imago Dei,* Bavinck writes:

> The idea is not that man has been created in correspondence to something that is in God which is called image and likeness of God, such as, for instance, the Son. Rather, man has been so created that he is in very truth *imago Dei.* Moreover, this creation in God's image is in no sense limited either with respect to the Original or with respect to the human reflection. It is not said that man has only some qualities of the divine being, or that he has been created in the image of one of the Persons of the Trinity. Nor is it said that man is only partially image of God, be it soul or intellect or holiness. To the contrary, it is the whole man who is image of the whole Deity.[5]

To be sure, Bavinck, too, has problems relating the image of God after the fall to the image in its unviolated integrity. He distinguishes between image in the "narrower sense" and in the "broader sense." Sin has brought about the loss of the former and the corruption of the latter, but the narrower and broader senses do not register on the reader as "parts" of an indivisible entity. In his lengthy discussion it is often quite impossible to determine whether he is speaking about the state of the image in its integrity or in its fallen condition. Unlike Calvin he is less disposed to systematize the limited available data into exclu-

5. Herman Bavinck, *Gereformeerde Dogmatiek,* 2d and enlarged ed., 4 vols. (Kampen: J. H. Kok, 1908), 2:569.

sive concepts and more inclined to express himself in terms of the language of Scripture, as in Genesis 9:6 and James 3:9. The retention of the mystical and the recognition of the limits of revelation are notable features in all of Bavinck's dogmatic expositions.

> Nothing of the image of God is excluded from man's being. All creatures reveal *vestigia Dei.* Man is *imago Dei.* And he is that altogether and completely, in soul and body, in all its faculties and powers, in all circumstances and relationships. Man is the image of God because and insofar as he is truly human. And he is human, truly and really human, because and in the same measure that he is image of God. . . . The Bible would not be able to speak about God in human terms and apply to him all manner of human attributes had God not made man fully in his own image in the first place. It is the task of Christian theology to set forth this divine image in the whole of man's being.[6]

Finally, but importantly, we must call attention to the justly famous third chapter of Book I of Calvin's *Institutes,* "The Knowledge of God Has Been Naturally Implanted in the Minds of Men." There is, says Calvin, "within the human mind, and indeed by natural instinct, an awareness of divinity." If ignorance of God is to be looked for anywhere,

> surely one is most likely to find an example of it among the more backward folk and those more remote from civilization. Yet there is, as the eminent pagan says, no nation so barbarous, no people so savage, that they have not a deep-seated conviction that there is a God. And they who in other aspects of life seem least to differ from brutes still continue to retain some seed of religion. So deeply does the common conception occupy the minds of all, so tenaciously does it inhere in the hearts of all! Therefore, since from the beginning of the world there has been no region, no city, in short, no household, that could do without religion, there lies in this a tacit confession of a sense of deity inscribed in the hearts of all. (I.iii.1)

6. Bavinck, *Gereformeerde Dogmatiek,* p. 597.

This sense of deity *(sensus divinitatis)* which Calvin also calls seed of religion *(semen religionis)* is therefore a universally and at all times active "natural instinct" which is "naturally implanted" in the human mind. Presumably, therefore, it is an essential aspect of the *imago Dei* in Man. Indeed, this aspect of the image affects the life of mankind more deeply than do those natural gifts reflecting the image of God in "earthly things." In the West, Calvin's "liberal arts" would appear to have triumphed over the *sensus divinitatis.* But the West is not the whole of mankind. Precisely when secularized Western man thought he had the world well under control, Islam and Hinduism raised their languid selves after World War II, cast out their colonial masters, reasserted their ancient religious traditions, and radically affected the international scene at crucial levels.

Calvin is quite correct to point out in subsequent chapters how self-destructively men hold down within themselves this sense of divinity, or ignore the evidence of its truth in the mighty powers of nature around them which point to the Creator. But it is not at all clear why this sense of divinity is (as must be supposed without a clear statement to the contrary) subsumed under that part of the image of God which reflects the "earthly things." It seems wholly arbitrary to say that the *sensus divinitatis* is "naturally implanted," that it is a part of our "natural" being and therefore presumably not a reflection in Man of the "heavenly things." True, the sense of divinity is suppressed in unrighteousness. But neither do men honor God in the many "excellent gifts" that have been bestowed on them for earthly usefulness. On the contrary, Calvin states, their use of the gifts without recognition of the Giver turns this use into sin, for which punishment is proper. The *sensus divinitatis* is a reflection in man of God's "Godness," so to speak, and there is no reality in the whole creation that constitutes a greater distortion of a heavenly gift than Man's response to the awareness of his Maker given him at his creation. On what ground can it be denied that the *sensus divinitatis* is a spark or remnant of the "heavenly things"?

Thus I would argue that the simultaneous existence in all

men of this sense of the divine and of its gross misreading is the clearest evidence of the remnant or spark of the image of God originally given and of Man's suppression of the light vouchsafed to him in his alienation from the heart of God. In short, the glimmer, the residuum, the remnant, the spark of the image of God in its integrity is a glimmer, a residuum, a remnant, a spark of the one and undivided Light and Life and Being of God the Creator, through which Man continues to witness to him even in his condition of darkness and estrangement from the Source of his life.

Whether we speak here of "spark" and "glimmer," suggesting the idea of irreducible minuteness, or of "residuum" and "remnant," implying a somewhat larger substantiality, makes no difference. A spark can start a forest fire. Faith like a mustard seed can remove mountains. The life of God does not depend on its quantity but on its actuality, its reality, its authenticity.

In view of these considerations, the expression "total depravity" as applied to Man must be viewed as biblically, religiously, and theologically untenable. It takes the Christian conception of sin an unwarranted step beyond the biblically permissible boundary. It heavily encumbers the missionary witness of the church by denying to it the indispensable element of the "point of contact" with the hearer. It requires doing violence to the text of Scripture to provide it with theological validity. Not least, it calls forth a theological antidote which we must examine in the next chapter.

Chapter IV

Why "Common Grace"?

When Gentiles who have not the law do by nature what the law requires, they are a law to themselves, even though they do not have the law.

Romans 2:14

Reformed theology has from the beginning been troubled by a dilemma it can neither resolve nor disregard. On the one hand, it affirms as a cornerstone doctrine that Man is totally depraved; on the other, it must somehow account for the tremendous amount of good that our allegedly depraved humanity is able to perform. When the indisputable facts of life contradict an alleged teaching of Scripture, we must modify our understanding of either the teaching or of the facts we observe. The evil that engulfs society, from petty bribe to nuclear destruction, is easily explained by the theory of total depravity. The good in society, from the cup of cold water given to a thirsty person to famine relief on an intercontinental scale, is explainable on a Reformed basis only in terms of artificial constructions.

This either-or reasoning has never been accepted by the Reformed theological community. Its force, however, has never been ignored either. Reformed theology has seen a problem here, but it has always viewed it as manageable. We have considered Calvin's handling of it. Unregenerate Man can do nothing that is good in the sight of God. All of Man's "goodness" flows from minds that "remain enveloped in hypocrisy and deceitful craft and [from] hearts bound by inner perversity." This, as we have seen, is hardly convincing.

A more reasonable effort to resolve the problem was made by Abraham Kuyper, the influential theologian and social reformer in the Netherlands from the 1870s to the second decade of the twentieth century. He accepted the doctrine of total depravity and as a consequence posited an absolute "antithesis" between the kingdom of God and the kingdom of Man, between believer and unbeliever, between church and world. The spiritual lives of the two parties to the antithesis moved in mutually exclusive realms. But how can two walk together socially and politically unless they agree? How can adherents of a Calvinistic world-and-life view work together with others in national forums and jurisdictions and programs for the common good?

Kuyper judged he had found a basis for this in the doctrine of common grace. He found in the universal blessings of natural life—rain and sunshine, health and family, social coherence, the gifts of intellect, feeling, and will—a basis from which people of varying background, not least religiously, could work together in the national interest. Like saving or "special" grace, this universal endowment or "common" grace was also an undeserved and forfeited good. It was this that warranted the use of the word "grace." It was a post-fall bestowal on totally depraved humanity to make possible a functioning society of people all of whom were by nature totally depraved. Indeed, God's common grace had the deeper purpose of providing a river bed for the flow of history in which the redemptive plan of God would be channeled and brought to consummation.

The terms "common grace" and "special grace" leave the impression that the distinctive feature of each is marked by the adjective. All receive a grace that is "common"; some receive in addition a grace that is "special." Some therefore partake of two graces, all others of one. Judging by the simple sound of the two expressions, one might conclude that they are basically similar. Just as a stadium has open seats and reserved seats, so there are two kinds of grace, common and special. The latter is a sort of refinement or enhancement of the former, which a favored group receives in addition to the general distribution. As general stores and hardware stores have basically similar functions, namely to trade in articles commercially, so the two graces must have similar purposes.

The comparison points up a factor of which Reformed theology has taken inadequate note, namely the fundamental impropriety of calling "common grace" *grace.* The difference between the two graces is nothing less than extraordinary. They share a purely formal characteristic: both represent a bestowal of forfeited divine favor on humanity. For the rest they are disparate in all respects. The special grace of God is concerned solely and exclusively with a dimension of Man's relationship to God that was inconceivable before the fall. It forms no part whatever of the vast whole that God's six great creative acts brought into being at the birth of time. It refers solely to a cosmic rescue operation, which was in no way envisioned in the creation of all that is. That is why St. Paul designates the saving work of God in Christ as a "new creation" (2 Cor. 5:17).

True, there is a general benevolence of God to all his creatures, and some may choose to call this grace. For example, Article XIII of the sixteenth-century Belgic Confession speaks of the unfallen angels as those who "have by the grace of God remained in their first state." But this is an exceptional use of the word. In Reformed theology both special grace and common grace point to the goodness or benevolence of God as dimensions that came into being after the fall of Man into sin.

Beyond question this is correct with respect to the saving power of God (i.e., special or redemptive grace) adumbrated in Genesis 3:15. It represents a clear and abrupt intervention of God in the life of Man and of his world, an intervention which had no background other than God's gracious will. On it creation sheds no light.

In Reformed theology, common grace functions to hold creation intact during the long interval in which special grace works out its purposes. In the post-fall world the entire creation continues to exist. The world of nature is the stage on which the human drama—that is, the drama of the *imago Dei*—plays itself out. But both the stage and the drama are entirely within the cosmos. Both are concerned with the "natural world," and therefore with all that is good and evil in human history. In this drama, common grace sustains all that is ennobling and serves as restraint on and palliative for all that is degrading.

By using the term "common grace" as it does, Reformed theology is in effect saying that history is grace, that the social order and the political order and the economic order and the schools and universities, procreation, the arts, the weather, agriculture, manufacturing, oceanography, and the police are all "grace." It is somewhat akin to the broad usage sometimes given to the word *sacramental*, which often tends to detract from the beauty, depth, and meaning of baptism and the Lord's Supper.

This, however, is not the meaning that overwhelmingly marks the use of the word *grace* (Greek: *charis*) in the New Testament. There it appears as a unitary and integrating principle underlying all the manifestations of the power of God in the salvation of Man from sin. The nuances are many but the work is one. Grace and truth came by Jesus Christ (John 1:17); the apostles bore witness to the word of God's grace (Acts 13:43); the congregation is greeted with the epistolary salutation, "Grace to you and peace from God our Father and the Lord Jesus Christ" (Rom. 1:7); if many died through one man's trespass, much more has the grace of that one man Jesus Christ abounded for many (Rom. 5:15); sin shall have no dominion over believers for they are not under law but under grace (Rom. 6:14); there is a remnant chosen by grace, but if it is by grace, it is no longer on the basis of works; otherwise grace would no longer be grace (Rom. 11:5-6); the grace of God has appeared for the salvation of all men (Titus

2:11). This list could be greatly extended, but it suffices to illustrate both the unity of the dimension called grace and the multiform expression it finds in the believing community.

In a few New Testament passages, *charis* is used for a disposition of people to people in everyday matters; and it is then translated "favor." After Pentecost the believers found "favor with all the people" (Acts 2:47); in Stephen's speech before the Jewish council he referred to Joseph as enjoying "favor and wisdom before Pharaoh, king of Egypt" (Acts 7:10). Felix, "desiring to do the Jews a favor," left Paul in prison (Acts 24:27), and the chief priests and principal men of the Jews asked his successor, Festus, to have Paul sent to Jerusalem "as a favor" to them (Acts 25:3). But when God shows *charis*, it is with redemptive intent, as the evangelical world understands the word *redemptive.*

In the Old Testament the characteristic word for grace or favor in the sense of God's saving disposition and deeds is the Hebrew word *chen.* It is also, however, widely used to indicate favor shown on the purely horizontal level. The New Testament takes the Greek equivalent and narrows its use almost exclusively to the goodness of God mediated to people through the saving work of Christ. The Greek word for gift *(charisma)* is in the New Testament used only for bestowals in a spiritual context.

By questioning the propriety of describing as "grace" God's general goodness to all under the condition of sin, albeit "common" grace, we are not concerned about the mere use of a word. Kindness, benefaction, patience, forbearance, or goodwill could be used to convey the same idea; and adding "grace" to this list in the sense of Old Testament usage is not in itself objectionable. The point at issue is quite different and far reaching.

The difficulty with the doctrine of common grace in Reformed theology is twofold. First, what Reformed theology most insistently alleges Man to be, namely totally depraved, is a state or condition of his existence which because of common grace never comes to view. Second, the doctrine of common grace sidelines the image of God concept as an effective force in the life of Man in the state of sin. We address ourselves to each in turn.

The Bible presents four classes of historical humanity: Man in the state of integrity, Man as fallen, Man as redeemed, and Man as glorified. In all of these Man is a concrete, living, tangible, visible, active human entity: in Adam and Eve in the state of rectitude, in them and in their posterity after the fall, in the saints as redeemed from the fall, and in Christ, our forerunner, risen and ascended to heaven.

The Reformed theological tradition, while sincerely believing this, has done so with a mental reservation that the rest of the church does not have. It believes that the concrete, living, visible humanity of which it is a part, though truly fallen into total depravity, is in actual fact a cosmeticized humanity, whose true face is never seen. The only concrete, living, visible humanity that can ever be seen is "common grace" humanity. The *real* fallen humanity is the *totally depraved* humanity. But *that* humanity is in Reformed theology a one hundred percent abstraction. When Man fell into his alleged total depravity, he fell—without any intervening period whatever—into the restraining and the favoring arms of common grace.

In Reformed theology common grace informs every post-fall human being, it enfolds the whole of humanity, and that humanity conditioned by common grace is the *only* humanity that has ever lived or ever will live on this side of eternity. There is no other. No person has ever, in the experienced reality of life, been totally depraved. Who can deny that there have been and are horrible examples of human depravity, individually and collectively? But no Reformed theologian would dare to affirm that even these wretched examplars of human wickedness were utterly bereft of common-grace goodness. The idea of a totally depraved humanity always hovers in the Reformed theological mind as a disembodied specter that it can never come to grips with.

Some have tried to take the sharpest sting out of "total depravity" by positing an even lower form of sinfulness called "absolute depravity." But this is inherently impossible. The state of "absolute" depravity would deprive a person of participation in the image of God, so that the category of humanity would cease to apply. Where the image of God exists, there cannot fail to be some manifestation of goodness, however small. There can be degrees of totality—greater or less, broader or narrower pervasiveness of evil. But "absolute" knows no degrees.

The particular penalties laid upon Adam and Eve indicate God's displeasure, but far from indicating Man's being thrust into total depravity of life, they are generally understood as symbolizing the manifold suffering he would encounter along life's journey. There is no indication of Man's being deprived of the image of God in the post-fall state, though the divine displeasure and Man's expulsion from the garden make it quite clear that the *imago* was greatly damaged. We understand this damage as a radical disorientation of Man's creationally given relationship to God, to the surrounding world, to fellow man, and to himself. His retention of the image, regardless of its orientation, is indicated by the declaration in Genesis 9:6 that "whoever sheds the blood of man, by man shall his blood be shed; for God made man in his own image," and in the overtones of Psalm 8.

An equally disturbing negative effect of the doctrine of common grace is its sidelining of the scriptural teaching concerning Man as the image of God. As image of God, however deeply fallen, Man retained all the relationships in which he had been created, as noted above. His formal relational situation after the fall is identical with that before the fall. It is not these relationships by themselves that constitute Man as image of God. Animals also stand in relationship to God, to other animals, to themselves, and to their world. But they are not aware of this in the same self-conscious and responsible manner as Man. For this reason they are more aptly described as *vestigia Dei,*[1] whereas Man is *imago Dei.*

1. For St. Augustine's use of this term see Chapter 1, page 13ff.

The relationships in which Man stands receive their concrete significance from his having been created to be a *likeness* of God. That is to say, paradoxically, Man is a created divinity, a literal and true *image* of God the Creator of heaven and earth. One could almost say that the difference between God and Man is one of degree—of infinite degree, to be sure, but of degree—except for one comprehensive factor that shatters any such comparison: God is *autonomous,* a law to himself, therefore self-sufficient, self-contained, self-determined, independent. Whatever the similarity of Man to God, it is absolutely qualified by the fact that, in distinction from the autonomy of God, Man is *heteronomous,* under other law than his own. Man is conditioned by, subordinate to, dependent upon a Power outside himself. The glory of God is his autonomy; the glory of Man is his heteronomy. By "glory" here we mean the grandeur, the pride, the nobility, the splendor, the magnificence, the fullness, the radiance, the genuineness, the authenticity—of God in his autonomy and of Man in his dependency.

That this is true of God is, of course, beyond all dispute. God is God, and with him is all power. He is the Creator, and in him all things live and move and have their being. Our faith teaches us also to speak highly of ourselves in our heteronomous dependence on the great Other; and the believer's conscious experience of life makes this a glad confession. To say that the pinnacle of our self-realization, the highest fulfillment of our humanity, lies in dependence on and service to God is one thing. To say that the same is true with respect to our dependence on and service to "the other" or to "others," let alone "the world"—that is a different matter. It requires a larger measure of grace than we appear to have capacity for to be able genuinely to say this and concretely to live what we affirm. Yet such is the dominical and the apostolic teaching and example.

This shortcoming reveals how deeply we have fallen from our first estate: "whoever would be great among you must be your servant, and whoever would be first among you must be your slave; even as the Son of man came not to be served but to serve, and to give his life as a ransom for many" (Matt. 20:26-28). "For which is the greater, one who sits at table, or one who serves? Is it not the one who sits at table? But I am among you as one who serves" (Luke 22:27). And again, whoever humbles himself like a child "is the greatest in the kingdom of heaven" (Matt. 18:4). Like the Lord's, so is the apostle's teaching: "Do nothing from selfishness or conceit, but in humility count others better than yourselves." We must look not only to our own interests, but also to the interests of others, having this mind in us, which was also in Christ, who, being found in human form though equal with God, "humbled himself and became obedient unto death, even death on a cross" (Phil. 2:3-8). And, "you know the grace of our Lord Jesus Christ, that though he was rich, yet for your sake he became poor, so that by his poverty you might become rich" (2 Cor. 8:9).

Our horizontal relationships test the sincerity of the professed priority of God in our lives. It is the test of loving the neighbor as we love ourselves. We are born to love ourselves with strong devotion. Our temptation is first of all to satisfy *our* wants, fulfill *our* desires, and meet *our* needs, as *we* see them. Even those who prefer anonymity to recognition, who seek to achieve their purposes quietly and practice self-effacement as a policy, may be as selfish as those who overtly seek their own ends. Too often our genuinely heteronomous service to God, to others, and to the world around us atrophies in the competing autonomous zeal for self. And often we recruit religion—and thereby God himself—into our quest for autonomous power and fulfillment.

Here both the nature and the scope of the distortion of the image of God become evident. Not only do we stand in four relationships, one vertical and three horizontal. Not only is the vertical relationship basic to the other three. But our relationship to God permeates and informs our horizontal relationships. We cannot meet the neighbor without meeting God; we cannot lose ourselves in the world without being surrounded by his presence; and least of all can we deal with ourselves without facing him in whose image we are made.

These circumstances undercut the comfortable secular premise that eliminating religion from life leaves all other areas untouched. "Whither shall I go from thy Spirit? Or whither shall I flee from thy presence? If I ascend to heaven, thou art there! If I make my bed in Sheol, thou art there!" (Ps. 139:7-8). It is striking how Jesus' parables use the dynamics of horizontal relationships to illustrate the reality of the vertical. Paul makes classic use of the natural creation to confront Man with his Maker:

> For the wrath of God is revealed from heaven against all ungodliness and wickedness of men who by their wickedness suppress the truth. For what can be known about God is plain to them, because God has shown it to them. Ever since the creation of the world his invisible nature, namely, his eternal power and deity, has been clearly perceived in the things that have been made. So they are without excuse. (Rom. 1:18-20)

The basic sin of Man created for heteronomy is the unashamed assertion of autonomy. This affirmation of what he is not and does not have is at the same time a denial of what he is and has, namely his image-being and his image-character. In this autonomy he glories even though bloodied beyond recognition by the irresolvable conflicts and contradictions into which it casts him. Israel was both a contemporary and a prophetic picture of him: "The whole head is sick, and the whole heart faint. From the sole of the foot even to the head, there is no soundness in it, but bruises and sores and bleeding wounds" (Isa. 1:5-6). Fish in the water and birds in the air are gloriously free in the elements that unconditionally confine them, but Man, devoid of their creaturely wisdom, says of both Creator and Redeemer, "Let us burst their bonds asunder, and cast their cords from us" (Ps. 2:3).

"Invictus" by William Ernest Henley is the incomparable poetic expression of the pathetic courage which this misreading of reality inspires.

> Out of the night that covers me,
> Black as the Pit from pole to pole,

I thank whatever gods may be
For my unconquerable soul. . . .

It matters not how strait the gate,
How charged with punishments the scroll,
I am the master of my fate;
I am the captain of my soul.

The yoke God lays upon Man restored to heteronomic sanity is easy, and its burden is light. Lacking this reconstitution in right-mindedness, however, autonomic folly sends him stumbling down the dismal avenues of the nuclear age, the demonstration par excellence of endowment in knowledge, wisdom, and ingenuity gone mad—all at the hands of the elite in science, education, industry, and government, who are honored as pillars of society.

The Bible designates the repudiation of heteronomy by autonomous Man with one simple word: *sin.* One can sin against one's neighbor, or against the laws or mores of the community, or against one's conscience, but only in a derived way. The word *sin* foremost and always states or implies a guilty *vertical* relationship. The great penitential prayer of David in Psalm 51 reveals this basic principle in the human-divine relationship. It was written after Nathan the prophet had come to David and with his burning "You are the man" turned David's royal indignation against himself (2 Sam. 12:1-10). Then, standing in the guilt of his callous military murder of Uriah and calculated adultery with Uriah's wife Bathsheba, David confessed to God, "Against thee, thee only, have I sinned" (Ps. 51:4).

In his cruelty, in his ruthlessness and inhumanity, in his lust, David had met God in his victims, and against him was his sin. So basic is Man's relationship to God that he stands in it even in his horizontal relationships.

Remarkably, in our highly secular age, the true meaning of the word *sin* has been retained with only minor dilution, in dictionary definition: Merriam Webster's *New Collegiate Dictionary* defines sin as "an offense against religious or moral law";

"transgression of the law of God"; "a vitiated state of human nature in which the self is estranged from God." A concession to the horizontal is "an action that is or is felt to be highly reprehensible [such as] 'it's a sin to waste food.'"

Man's God-relatedness is a bond he cannot break. Religious Man in his estrangement from the true God finds other gods to worship. Secular Man in his God-less world finds "causes" to serve or "ideals" to uphold. In nine cases out of ten, no Christian would take issue either with the causes or the ideals. The sin is giving to them the place of God in the life of Man. "Our souls are restless," said St. Augustine, "until they rest in thee." Man cannot escape the recollection of him in whose image he was made and in whom alone life has meaning. But all his straining cannot undo the alienation that bars the way to the fellowship—horizontal *and* vertical—in which and for which he was created. Though he comes before God with the contemporary equivalent of burnt offerings of calves a year old, thousands of rams, and ten thousands of rivers of oil, these cannot remove the stain of guilt and the pain of loneliness in his soul.

> He has showed you, O man, what is good;
> and what does the Lord require of you
> but to do justice, and to love kindness,
> and to walk humbly with your God? (Mic. 6:8)

But where shall we find the power to be just, to love kindness, to walk humbly with God when every human being is in himself an autonomous entity who is often very willing to be just and to love kindness, but insists on walking only with himself—and seldom with humility?

In our effort to find the theological answer to this question, we must seek first to understand how to view unredeemed fallen Man in terms of the image of God concept *without* the notion of total depravity and therefore *without* the mitigating palliative of common grace.

The position of this book is basically that "Man" (in the sense of mankind, humanity) and "image of God" are completely convertible or synonymous expressions. Man or image of God *before* the fall was Man or image of God in fellowship (with God, with fellow man, with the world, and with himself). Man or image of God *after* the fall is Man or image of God in alienation (from God, from fellow man, from the world, and from himself). The condition of Man in these two states of his existence can also be indicated in other ways: innocence *vs.* guilt, holiness *vs.* sin, integrity *vs.* curse, light *vs.* darkness, life *vs.* death, other-centeredness *vs.* self-centeredness, or, as we have considered at some length above, heteronomy *vs.* autonomy. What Man was in his pre-fall condition, whether in terms of fellowship, holiness, integrity, innocence, light, life, or heteronomy, he was in the fullness of these qualities. No qualification detracted from the wholeness or health of the excellence that characterized Man's pre-fall state. All that God had made, not least his own image Man, was "good," even "very good" (Gen. 1:31).

This goodness was, moreover, subject to one very positive qualification: it could grow, it could develop, it could expand. However much it may have been expressed already before the fall, it was a reality with limitless potential for elaboration, adaptation, and refinement. As the life of the Creator is not static but active, so the life of his deputy on earth was imbued with vitality, moving on to ever new and enlarged deployment of innately bestowed gifts and powers.

As unfallen Man was thus qualified in the direction of ever-increasing enrichment of his gifts, so fallen Man retains both a certain goodness and a capacity for the development of his gifts. But these qualities are residual, remnants of the image in which he was created. Moreover, as remainders they stand in the context of his disoriented relationships to God, to self, to the neighbor, and to the world around him. Far from being a post-fall bestowal, therefore, they constitute a direct continuation of Man's pre-fall condition, but in a seriously debilitated and diminished state.

Such is the image of God under the condition of sin. Such is Man; such is the human race. By the simple fact of birth, every human being individually and every generation collectively enter upon the burden of sin, infirmity, and alienation. We are not speaking here of the effect redemption has on this condition, but only of the situation that in principle came into being through the fall of Man and cannot be turned around by any human exertion or be healed by any power within the vast created cosmos. We speak of Man as he is, of Man as he is in his goodness and as he is in his potential for goodness. We speak of Man as he is in his evil and as he is in his potential for evil. We speak of Man after he had exchanged life for death as the ultimate condition of his existence.

This admixture of good and evil in Man is so profound, so complex, so all-pervasive that sorting out the one from the other is more often than not impossible. They seem to be not only mutually present everywhere, but also mutually interpenetrative. The growth, development, and consequent complexity of the human situation has been so great, multiplied geometrically generation after generation, that no clear analysis of their respective limits is possible. The basic factors of environment and heredity alone are incalculable in their effects. But to these must be added the seldom considered circumstance that every human being, besides being a product of heredity and environment, is also a product of his own individuality. This individuality, perhaps best expressed in the concept of "person," while channeled into being by heredity and environment, is not fully accounted for by either. Every human being is *sui generis* while at the same time fully member of the society of Man, which is the *imago Dei* writ large. The nature of that society is to be collectively, wholly, and organically one, and in its individual membership wholly and organically diverse.

The entrance of sin into the life of Man was the intrusion of evil into a being who was good. The good has independent existence; evil does not. It is always parasitic. Truth can stand by itself; the lie always needs a basis of truth in order to be. The lie—or, more comprehensively, evil—is therefore always inseparably linked to the truth, or goodness. This linkage constitutes a restraint on it that never ceases to be in some measure effective; and the good in that linkage is always a force that, under given circumstances, can expand and assert itself with irresistible power.

The effect of sin on the image was to distort it. It could not destroy it. An essential condition of its existence is to be limited by the good. An essential condition of its existence is also to be, in however ultimate a sense, incidental. Sin is not an integral part of God's created work. It came into the structure of creation, as it were, on the side. Therefore it can be removed like a splinter from the flesh or an irritant from the eye.

When Man fell, therefore, he, in retaining his status as *imago Dei,* carried with him his own restraint on the evil he had embraced.

> When Gentiles who have not the law do by nature what the law requires, they are a law to themselves, even though they do not have the law. They show that what the law requires is written on their hearts, while their conscience also bears witness and their conflicting thoughts accuse or perhaps excuse them. (Rom. 2:14-15)

In no way do I understand this gift of conscience among people who have never heard the gospel to be a bestowal of "common grace" after the fall had taken place. They do what the law requires "by nature." By what nature? By a new nature or an additional nature conferred by common grace? No, God continues to deal with the very same *imago* person after the fall as he did before, but now with a *sinful image.* The father continued to yearn for the prodigal's return as the same son who had left him. The father-son relationship had never been cluttered up with a "common grace" interlude.

Reformed theology, while acknowledging Man as continuing to be *imago Dei,* has failed to regard the *imago* aspect of Man's being as the basis of all restraint on sin in his life. Instead, constrained by its preoccupation with "total depravity," it conceived an assumed "grace," forgetting that sin, by lodging itself in the soul of Man, thus became bound to the residual image of

God in that soul, which could never fail in greater or less measure to limit the power of evil.

Man's weapon against sin is not an artificial "common grace" granted to him as a post-fall bestowal. It is rather that very human entity which he himself is, who in his fall in Adam retained his creational structure, albeit with a greatly impaired but still functional dynamic, namely *the reduction of the image of God in which he had been created.*

By taking seriously the *imago* concept as a principle governing far more theological territory than is usually associated with it, we have in this and in the preceding chapter gained two new perspectives. The first is that the traditional Reformed concept of "total depravity" is a theological abstraction without content in real life and an indefensible overstatement of the sinfulness of Man. The second is that the term "common grace" is not only an artificial explanation of the good that characterizes the life of Man in his fallen state, but also a sort of pretender, acting out a role in theology that belongs exclusively to existential, here and now, fallen Man, the *imago Dei,* Man as he is in his sin without any admixture of a mitigating, divinely bestowed post-fall endowment. This brings with it the very real gain of seeing *grace* again as it is throughout the New Testament, unburdened by the qualifying adjective "common" and therefore unburdened by the quite superfluous adjective "special."

We must inquire next into Man's capacity as *imago Dei* for knowledge of and faith in God. That is, how can Man, fallen and, in the Pauline sense, "dead in sins and trespasses," come again to know and fear God with filial understanding and affection? How can he achieve the fulfillment of all for which he was created and thus at last find peace with God, with fellow man, with his environing world, and with himself?

Chapter V

The Responding *Imago*

> *Get yourselves a new heart and a new spirit! Why will you die, O house of Israel?*
>
> Ezekiel 18:31

When Man the creature lives under the government of a Creator who is not also for him a Redeemer, he lives in a self-made prison. Man's alienation from God, bringing in its wake alienation from the neighbor, from the environing world, and even from himself, has turned the freedom given with his creation into bondage. In remaining true to his autonomous self, he rejects as untrue and therefore unacceptable his creationally given status as steward who, while owning nothing, is nevertheless, under God, lord of all he surveys.

There is no provision within the confines of creation, and thus within Man's resources, for achieving a fruitful working relationship between the self, the neighbor, and the surrounding world if within that creation the sovereign lordship of the Creator is denied. Apart from the decisive stabilizing and meaning-giving verticality of his relationship to God, *on God's terms*, there is no way in which the creature called Man can shuffle the components of creation so as to form a harmonious horizontality.

The depth and extent of Man's defection is all the more profound because he is, as has been said, "inalienably religious." Created in him, as an inherent aspect of his being, was a *sensus divinitatis*—a feeling for, an affinity with, an awareness of the divine. Man can no more escape his created relationship to God than he can his shadow. Yet, because of his decision to go it alone, this religious sense is no longer able to fix on the Creator. Upon what then does the religious sensibility of unredeemed Man focus? It fashions in one way or another gods of its own devising in the form of the sin of idolatry, denounced throughout the Bible.

Man's capacity for God is thus filled with non-God, by the very gift that made Man to be image of God. For this reason, within the whole of creation, there is no way back to God for Man as self-constituted autonomous creature. His search to satisfy the ingrained desire for fellowship with a power beyond himself can only lay hold of one or another *ersatz* god, whether an amulet, a carved image, corporate power, a Porsche, a noble ideal to the service of which he may devote his whole life, or a refined intellectual concept of deity like Aristotle's Unmoved Mover.

Scripture teaches that Man's predicament is such that his alienation from God can be removed only by God himself. The Creator must become Redeemer. This means specifically that the Creator cannot save Man and the world that fell with him within means given by any earthly reality or by any provision that went into the creation of the universe. Creation did not have built into it some sort of insurance against the catastrophe of human revolt. After that catastrophe happened, it could only be neutralized or overcome by some power that was not inherent in creation while yet being wholly consonant with the character of the Creator—and therefore also compatible with the character of Man as *imago Dei.*

A wholly new dimension of relationship between God and Man had to be brought into being which, while flowing out of the heart of the Creator God, would be redemptive rather than creational in character. This wholly new dimension is called "the grace of our Lord Jesus Christ." As Hebrews 9:11-12 puts it, "But when Christ appeared as a high priest of the good things that have come, then through the greater and more perfect tent (not made with hands, that is, *not of this creation*) he entered once for all into the Holy Place" (italics added).

No Christian theological tradition sets forth this message more clearly and unambiguously than that of the Reformed churches. Their message is that salvation is by grace alone. It is not effected by Man, but by God the Father through his Son incarnate, in the power of the Holy Spirit. This message contradicts every effort on the part of autonomous Man to effect reconciliation with God. It affirms that the salvation wrought by Christ through his life, death, and resurrection is a full and complete redemption which requires only the open heart and the outstretched hand of faith to be received—and even these are gifts of God. A remarkable aspect of the Reformed emphasis on ascribing salvation to the Creator who became Redeemer is the fruitful interaction to which this has led between creation and redemption in Reformed theology and life. The redemption of humanity stands in the foreground because of Man's headship in the world by virtue of his *imago* relationship to God. But redemption is not simply the redemption of humanity. The Redeemer envisages the redemption of the totality that he has made; and this vision must find a sort of firstfruits manifestation in the present dispensation.

But the fruitfulness with which the Reformed proclamation of the gospel has been adorned in its classic expression labors under a fearful disadvantage. This arises neither from the gospel nor from any legitimate deduction that may be made from it. Historically (and this history is important) the Reformed faith has taught—and in the minds of many continues to teach—that in the conception and intention of God the efficacy of the gospel is of limited extent. The life, death, and resurrection of Christ provide salvation only for a certain number of elect persons, and that number can be neither increased nor diminished. By an eternal decree that cannot be annulled or made of lesser effect, a segment of mankind called "the reprobate" are forever excluded from salvation. As the elect are destined forever to glorify God for his mercy, so the reprobate will through all eternity be a testimony to his justice.[1]

It is true that the doctrine of reprobation is seldom preached from Reformed pulpits. It is seldom discussed or written about as an aspect of Reformed piety. In Reformed creeds and Reformed theology all the emphasis falls on grace and little on the character, judgment, and fate of the reprobate. But in no way does this silence about or suppression of an undenied reality, never rejected no matter how horrible—Calvin called it a *decretum horribile* (*Institutes*, III.xxiii.7)— remove the Reformed embarrassment. So long as election in its classic formulation is held to refer to a fixed and unchangeable number of persons, there is a problem with those who do not belong to this number, whether they are called reprobate or, more euphemistically, "non-elect." What is their relationship to God's kingdom? What ultimate difference is there between reprobation and non-election?

The easiest and probably most common escape from this discomfiture is to ignore reprobation altogether. But such a course has the inevitable consequence of sharply playing down or forgetting about election. It is theologically pardonable to forget about reprobation because the Bible does not teach it. But it is theologically inexcusable to forget about or to downplay election, because the Bible teaches it plainly. The beginning of a solution is to realize that Reformed scholasticism is not the only way to read all that the Bible has to say about election. We shall address this question in a later chapter.[2] Here we are concerned with the relationship between faith and the image of God.

In the pre-fall condition of rectitude and innocence faith in God was not a problem. Man did not question his creaturely status, did not claim to be autonomous. Dependence on and trust in

1. Belgic Confession (1561), Article 16; Canons of Dort (1618-19), Articles 6, 7, and 15.

2. See Chapter 10 in its entirety.

God were part and parcel of his created being. There was fellowship between God and Man, and it was a fellowship not between equals but between Creator and creature, between the eternal divine Original and the time-conditioned human image. In the uncritical acceptance of this relationship lay Man's power, wisdom, majesty, happiness, and fruitfulness.

The question of faith became all-important in the condition of sin. How could Man's alienation from God be removed and replaced by the trust and fellowship in which he had been created? For Man *in his sin* to restore his relationship to God is inherently impossible because of his sin. His sinful nature drives him to and sustains him in the autonomy which contradicts the heteronomy in which he was made image of God. Man himself has been most wonderfully made, and he is surrounded by a natural world which is full of the majesty and glory of God. But he cannot see this as a marvelous work of the Creator whom he should in his beholding glorify. What he sees in creation is "Nature," a cosmic entity that somehow "came to be" apart from the will and might of a personal Creator-God. His disposition is to suppress the evidence before his eyes of the existence of this God.

Moreover, the natural creation no longer stands in its integrity. Sickness and death, famine and earthquakes, extremes of cold and heat, wars and social disharmony, the vulnerability of our faculties—all these provide rational grounds for seeing an evil as well as a good Power at the bottom of things; and Man has surrendered the spiritual discernment to distinguish between the two. His basic alienation from the Creator finds an echo in all his other relationships. The combination of sinful disposition and distorted situation inevitably leads to the suppression of the revelation of God that is within him as *imago Dei* and around him as *vestigia Dei.* That would seem to be the sense of St. Paul's testimony that men "by their wickedness suppress the truth" precisely in the context of their relation to the Creator's creation (Rom. 1:18-23).

How then do we enter into a relationship with God in which

it will again be possible to please him, to draw near to him and receive the reward of those who seek him? How can we draw near to God when our native inclination is to flee him? How can we seek him when our inmost being is spiritually geared to suppress the evidences of his existence? How can our proud autonomy be brought to surrender?

We begin our answer to this crucial question by noting that the relation between Redeemer and sinner is quite other than that between Creator and his *imago.* There is a difference between *being created* and *being redeemed* that bears fundamentally on how we are made members of the "new creation." In his creation Man was passive—if we may use that term for nonexistence prior to existence. Whether his creation is conceived as the consummation of a process or as an act by *fiat,* Man at no point existed as *imago Dei* prior to being so constituted by his Maker. By process or by act, God brought into existence from nonbeing a being with whom he was in full and unbroken fellowship from the first moment of Man's conscious existence. In the creation of this entity in its specific essence or nature as *imago Dei,* the *imago* played no role. In his relationship to God as *alter ego* he *was made;* he simply *became,* without the slightest contribution on his part.

In redemption the relation between Redeemer and sinner is wholly other. In that dimension the object of the Redeemer's outreach *exists.* Humanity exists as *imago Dei,* however fallen. God's address to fallen Man does not achieve its aim until he receives the *response* of assent and faith. In creation the relationship between God and Man was one of *making* and *being made*; in redemption the relationship is between *addressing* and *responding*—not between addressing and being addressed. The "being made" of creation brought into being the desired *alter ego,* God's *other self.* The "being addressed" of redemption does not in itself restore the fallen *alter ego* to fellowship. The human partner in the now-unhappy relationship must *respond.* That is to say, Man is active, profoundly involved, in his redemption.

In the whole first chapter of Genesis not a word or action by

Man is recorded. Yet the divine work was complete: "And God saw everything that he had made, and behold, it was very good" (Gen. 1:31). Quite the opposite is true in redemption. There the divine initiative is not complete until the hearer has responded to the proclaimed redemption and appropriated it in faith. This is not to say that God is dependent on Man for the success of his cosmic rescue mission. It is rather to say that textured into the warp and woof of God's redemption is the ineradicable and ever-determinative character of the *imago Dei,* with all the redemptive consequences that flow from that fact. In redemption Man *exists* as God's *alter ego,* albeit *fallen;* and the whole of the redemptive process is predicated on that basic creation-given, historically qualified reality.

Reformed theology has not only not honored this distinction but implicitly has condemned it. The Redeemer God intending reconciliation faces a situation substantively equivalent to that confronted by the Creator God in the work of creating. The Creator faced the fact of nonbeing; the Redeemer faces the fact of spiritual death in the form of unalterable alienation. This death constitutes the *nonexistence* of the condition required for the *response of faith.* If there is to be an affirmative response to the redemptive overture, the Redeemer must *create* it. There is in the existing humanity no point of contact or, as the German puts it, no *Anknüpfungspunkt,* literally, nothing to tie on to.

The point of contact according to Reformed teaching must be brought into being in Man by the equivalent of a divine creative act. Only *then* can Man become a responding subject. Without this the Redeemer can speak, can proclaim, can plead, can warn, can appeal, but the sinner cannot believe and be saved. He must *first* be born again, and in this rebirth he is as passive and spiritually nonexistent as Adam was before God formed him from the dust of the earth. The Redeemer effects the point of contact through the divine act of regeneration in as many individual cases as there are elect in the eternal counsel of God.

But does the *scriptural* idea of the image of God permit such a complete hiatus between God in his holiness and Man in his sin?

If in creating Man God did indeed bring into being an *alter ego,* a bosom companion, a friend who sticks closer than a brother, the fellowship between Creator God and creature Man must certainly express itself most fully and deeply in communion, in discourse, in mutual response. That, first and foremost, is where the depth and breadth of Man's humanity lie. There was in the beginning a point of contact for Man in God and in God for Man, because Man was created in the image of God, who is the divine Original, after which the human image was formed. For this reason God could see himself reflected in Man, and Man could find in God the infinitely larger self that underlay his own being. We may confidently say that speech and response between God and Man stand at the very heart of Man's being as *imago Dei.* It is no accident that the Son as image of the Father is called the *Word* of God. Only by means of words is it possible adequately to communicate as soul mates and speak from heart to heart.

The tragic interruption of this communication by reason of Man's sin did not altogether terminate it. The divine-human companionship now became divine-human confrontation. Yet from God's side, the longing for loving mutuality to be restored could break out touchingly: "Come now, let us reason together" (Isa. 1:18); and from Man's side there was a longing for fulfillment, inspired by God himself, that men "should seek God, in the hope that they might feel after him and find him" (Acts 17:27).

In no area of Reformed theology is the significance of Man's creation in the image of God more overlooked than in the matter of the point of contact in Man for the hearing and understanding of the gospel. The Reformed idea of a divine hidden agenda behind the calls to repentance and faith is thoroughly disqualified by Scripture's simple, artless, and insistent appeals and demands to do not only the obvious, but the necessary, the reasonable, the possible. Repent and believe the gospel! In all of the simple and direct prophetic, dominical, and apostolic calls to repentance and faith, the clear implication is this: You can if you will, for you have within you the resources to do the will of God. "If any man's will is to do his will, he shall know whether the teaching is from God or whether I am speaking on my own authority" (John 7:17). Consider the following passages:

> Turn to me and be saved, all the ends of the earth! (Isa. 45:22)
>
> Ho, every one who thirsts, come to the waters; and he who has no money, come, buy and eat! Come, buy wine and milk without money and without price. (Isa. 55:1)
>
> Return, faithless Israel, says the Lord. I will not look on you in anger, for I am merciful, says the Lord. (Jer. 3:12)
>
> I have sent to you all my servants the prophets . . . saying, 'Turn now every one of you from his evil way, and amend your doings.' (Jer. 35:15)
>
> Cast away from you all the transgressions which you have committed against me, and get yourselves a new heart and a new spirit! Why will you die, O house of Israel? (Ezek. 18:31)
>
> As I live, says the Lord God, I have no pleasure in the death of the wicked, but that the wicked turn from his way and live. (Ezek. 33:11)
>
> "Yet even now," says the Lord, "return to me with all your heart.". . . Return to the Lord, your God, for he is gracious and merciful. (Joel 2:12-13).
>
> Jonah . . . cried, "Yet forty days, and Nineveh shall be overthrown!" And the people of Nineveh believed God; they proclaimed a fast, and put on sackcloth. (Jon. 3:4-5)
>
> Come to me, all who labor and are heavy laden, and I will give you rest. Take my yoke upon you, and learn from me. . . . For my yoke is easy, and my burden is light. (Matt. 11:28-30)
>
> Repent therefore, and turn again, that your sins may be blotted out, that times of refreshing may come from the presence of the Lord. (Acts 3:19)
>
> The times of ignorance God overlooked, but now he commands all men everywhere to repent. (Acts 17:30)

> But how are men to call upon him in whom they have not believed? And how are they to believe in him of whom they have never heard? And how are they to hear without a preacher? And how can men preach unless they are sent? (Rom. 10:14-15)

> In Christ God was reconciling the world to himself, not counting their trespasses against them, and entrusting to us the message of reconciliation. . . . We beseech you on behalf of Christ, be reconciled to God. (2 Cor. 5:19-20)

> Behold, I stand at the door and knock; if any one hears my voice and opens the door, I will come in to him and eat with him, and he with me. (Rev. 3:20)

Are we to suppose that genuine, free, and willing response to these calls, warnings, admonitions, and exhortations could be made only by a certain unknown class of hearers or readers called "the elect"? Can it be that all others have a deceptive psychological freedom to obey, but are in fact bound by an eternal, irrevocable decree of God which unfailingly causes them to exercise their psychological freedom to believe or not to believe in the direction of unbelief?

The force of this question apparently overcame theological scruples even in the framing of the Canons of Dort, which declare that "As many as are called by the gospel are unfeignedly called. For God has most earnestly and truly declared in his Word what is acceptable to him, namely, that those who are called should come to him" (III-IV.8). The key word here, used three times, is "call." In the light of the following article, "call" here can mean no other than the simple, natural hearing of the gospel as preached. How can the reprobating God "unfeignedly" call those to faith concerning whom he has by an eternal decree determined "not to bestow upon them saving faith and the grace of conversion" (I.15)?

It is at this point that a serious concern with Man's creation in the image of God provides clear perspectives for removing this Reformed incongruity.

In the Reformed understanding of the ultimate renewal of

creation, the *imago Dei* as it *socially* came out of the hand of God the Creator is never in fact redeemed. *Individual members* of the human race are redeemed. The world of nature as a unitary entity, i.e., the *vestigia Dei,* is to be restored in all its fullness and splendor. The humanity that is the head of it is *not* so to be restored. Redemption, unlike creation, does not focus on a living unit called mankind, specifically the image of God as an organically integrated wholeness. It focuses on *individuals* called the elect.

By the common bond of spiritual rebirth these separate elect human entities are formed into a new unity variously termed the new humanity, the body of Christ, the church. Its members are interrelated as a community of saints honoring Christ, the last Adam, as their Head. In history the human race as the *imago Dei* generates its vast and varied offspring, which in their generations form the race of Man. But in the intention of God in ongoing history in principle, and altogether in the cosmic closing of the books in the Day of days, the human race, conceived and given being by the Creator as a unitary entity, will finally in the Reformed view break into two eternally irreconcilable segments: the elect and the non-elect—or, more credally speaking, the elect and the reprobate. It is not therefore *the tree of humanity* that is saved in its creation-given unity and solidarity. But this ill accords with Paul's inclusive vision: "For as in Adam all die, so also in Christ shall all be made alive" (1 Cor. 15:22). The "certain number" concept is so restrictive and exclusive that only a technical similarity would seem to be left of the corresponding magnitudes "in Adam" and "in Christ," and nothing whatever of the same "all" of which both are head.

When the significance of the difference between Man's *nonexistence* in God's act of creating and his *existence* in the act of redeeming is understood, the disastrous effect of not acknowledging it becomes evident. It means that then no organic continuity is seen between the old humanity and the new. It means failure to see that the biblical "new creation" is not *another* creation, that the "new man in Christ" is not a *different* person from the "old man in Adam." There is a powerful element of *continuity* between the created human *old* and the redeemed human *new,* but this uninterruptedness forms no part of the Reformed vision.

No clearer example of this can be found in the Bible than the conversion of Saul into Paul. All the power, religious fervor, and acuteness of mind that moved the enemy of the gospel to seek to destroy the church were now placed in its service. This constant element in Man, this bridge between the "old man" and the "new man," is the continued existence, whether in sinful rebellion or in saintly obedience, of the *imago Dei* in which God created the original Man. That *imago* has been damaged, disoriented, and distorted, but it has not been destroyed. By no means has it been reduced to becoming simply a channel of "common grace" to make it possible for "special grace" to effect redemptive ends. In the view here set forth the image of God is not only the *object* of the saving grace of Christ, it is in its very nature also and notably the *responding agent* to the grace of Christ.

In traditional teaching the Bible's pictorial or symbolic descriptions of sin and Man's recovery from it are given literal value. Dogmatically, expressions like "dead in sins and trespasses," "dead in your sins," "begetting," "born again," "new creation" are made to signify or to assume a state of spiritual impotence on the part of the sinner being addressed and thus total passivity in his reception of life in Christ by rebirth. Spoken to the unconverted, the gospel is not being addressed to the spiritually derailed and disoriented seeking fulfillment where it cannot be found, but to spiritual corpses.

The passage that immediately comes to mind here is Ezekiel's vision of the valley of dry bones. He is told to preach: "O dry bones, hear the word of the Lord." When he obeys this command, "there was a noise, . . . a rattling; and the bones came together, bone to its bone." As he looks, sinews and flesh come upon them and skin covers them, but there is no breath in them. Then God says to him, "Prophesy to the breath, prophesy, son of man, and say to the breath, Thus says the Lord God: Come from the four winds, O breath, and breathe upon these slain, that they may live." So he prophesies again "and the breath came into them, and they lived, and stood upon their feet, an exceedingly great host" (Ezek. 37:1-14).

What is forgotten in reading this vision is the quite different language of Ezekiel in chapter 18. There the same sinful Israel that is addressed as dried, disparate bones is told, "Repent and turn away from all your transgressions. . . . Cast away from you all the transgressions which you have committed against me, and get yourselves a new heart and a new spirit! Why will you die, O house of Israel?" (18:30-32). Here the living but spiritually dead are told to "get" a "new heart" and a "new spirit." Similarly, Paul writes to the Ephesians, "Awake, O sleeper, and arise from the dead" (5:14).

When Jesus told his disciples, "Truly, I say to you, unless you turn and become like children, you will never enter the kingdom of heaven" (Matt. 18:3), when he told Nicodemus, "Truly, truly, I say to you, unless one is born anew, he cannot see the kingdom of God" and "unless one is born of water and the Spirit, he cannot enter the kingdom of God. . . . Do not marvel that I said to you, you must be born anew" (John 3:3, 5, 7), was he telling them to effect their own rebirth? Was Ezekiel in substance telling Israel to do the same? From a traditional point of view, this is quite absurd. As a child cannot give birth to itself, so the spiritually dead cannot create a spiritually new self. Nevertheless, in Jesus' very conversation with Nicodemus, he spoke also these words, "And as Moses lifted up the serpent in the wilderness, so must the Son of man be lifted up, that whoever believes in him may have eternal life" (3:14-15). Then follows immediately the best-known verse in the Bible: "For God so loved the world that he gave his only Son, that whoever believes in him should not perish but have eternal life" (John 3:16).

Obviously, corpses and dry bones are not human beings. They no longer participate as living members in the human family and are therefore cut off from the *imago Dei* in which they had been created. For all that, Ezekiel's figure speaks a powerful truth: without the regenerating power of the Holy Spirit no flesh can be saved.

We must here face quite explicitly a central thesis of this book. It is that Man as *imago Dei*—and therefore all participants in the *imago,* that is, all members of the human race—has the competence to respond affirmatively to the proclamation of the gospel. Every hearer of the gospel has the spiritual resource to believe the gospel and become a living member of the body of Christ. In this sense, he can decide to be born again. At the same time, as we have said, Man as image of God *cannot* simply, in terms of power inherent in the structure of creation, without penetration by God as Redeemer, return to fellowship with the Creator. There is no possibility of self-salvation, there is no possibility of self-redemption. There is only the possibility of responding to a salvation already achieved, but not yet recognized and embraced. This possibility arises from the substratum of fallen Man's essential nature or being—his *existence* as *imago Dei.*

That Man as image of God retains a spark or glimmer or residuum of the full life given him in creation is unquestioned in all evangelical Christian theology. It is the existence of this life which constitutes Man as Man, which makes him human, which makes him the image of God. Sons or daughters in alienation from their parents do not cease to be the image of those who gave them birth, do not cease in their bodies, temperaments, and potentials to be extensions of the parental being. So, too, with Man in his relationship to God. He remains *imago Dei*—a fallen and sinful image, but also, by the grace of the Parent, a redeemable image, an offspring to which the parental heart stands open for forgiveness and reconciliation.

God's openness to Man, therefore, finds a corresponding feature in Man in the form of a capacity for God. This capacity is not localized in the mind or the heart or the will or the body. It is a quality of the whole, which is expressed in the fact of Man's humanity. It is humanness that sets Man apart from every other living being in the universe. And that humanness exists in all persons, because all partake of the life that is "the light of men," the light that glows in the darkness of every individual heart. It exists there because it has not been overcome or extinguished by the darkness of Man's alienation from it. It is the light "that enlightens every man . . . coming into the world" (John 1:9).This is the light that distinguishes a human being as *imago Dei* from the highest animal as *vestigium Dei.* In the state of integrity, this light fully illumined the whole Man—all his words, his deeds, his being. In the state of sin, this light is obscured, diminished, beclouded by Man's sinfulness and perverseness. But it is not extinguished. Indeed, on the purely horizontal level its rays shine out remarkably, yet so that their light, in the peculiar physics of the world of spiritual alienation, often serves to make the darkness more intense. But the light itself is light, however wrongly used, and the light is life, the light and the life of the Word of God through whom the world was made (John 1:1-5, 9). It is this light that constitutes *homo sapiens* as *imago Dei.*

With some oversimplification we may compare this light, as a small flame flickering in the human soul, to the pilot light in a gas range. The pilot light cannot of and by itself reach out to ignite the burners. It needs the infusion of gas to achieve this. Then it becomes the facilitator to effect the service of the range in all its functions.

After the fall, God has in his mercy permitted as it were a smoldering fire to remain as a witness to our creation in his image and its perpetuation in all generations of the human race. Kept from breaking into full and joyful flame by Man's alienation from God, it cannot rekindle the once-powerful fire that enlightened and energized the image which came forth from the heart and the hand of God in creation. But when the Christ-given Spirit, in the strength of his redemptive power, blows upon the sleeping fire, it can leap into flame and radiate again the entire being of the person.

The Old Testament history of the people of Israel foreshadowed the redemptive infusion of the Holy Spirit's power that was to come in the fullness of its time. In prophecy, in deeds and signs, in sacrifice and psaltery, in the Spirit's intermittent descents, God prepared the way for the fulfillment of Joel's vision: "And it shall come to pass afterward, that I will pour out my spirit on all flesh" (2:28). The cessation of God's direct universal concern with "the nations" in the calling of Abraham was not in fact an abrogation of concern. It was a strategic scaling down of redemptive solicitude to concentration on a small people. But that people was a representative people, holding in trust "the sonship, the glory, the covenants, the giving of the law, the worship, and the promises" (Rom. 9:4). The other nations were never lost to sight. Their day would come. " 'My name will be great among the nations, from the rising to the setting of the sun. In every place incense and pure offerings will be brought to my name, because my name will be great among the nations,' says the Lord Almighty" (Mal. 1:11).

However great the alienation of the nations from the Creator, the simple, unalterable fact of their humanity maintained in them a point of contact with God in the residual light of their fallen image of him. It awaited, unknown to them, the diffusion of God's direct redemptive concern to all the tribes and tongues and nations and peoples of the world. Until this time should be fulfilled, God's word to Israel was in its own way true of the glimmering of the divinely given light in the heart of all the world's peoples: "a bruised reed he will not break, and a dimly burning wick he will not quench. . . . He will not fail or be discouraged till he has established justice in the earth; and the coastlands wait for his law" (Isa. 42:3-4). The waiting came to an end on a day of a feast called Pentecost, on which occasion Jews scattered throughout the empire came to Jerusalem, the mother city.

On that day, in the most far-reaching and final representative event in the life of God's Old Testament people, the Holy Spirit was poured out on Jews from "every nation under heaven" (Acts 2:5). The fact that all to whom the Holy Spirit was given were devout Jews "from every nation under heaven" emphasizes its representative character all the more. In his sermon Peter cited in full Joel's great prophecy: "And in the last days it shall be, God declares, that I will pour out my Spirit upon all flesh. . . .

And it shall be that whoever calls on the name of the Lord shall be saved" (2:17, 21). At that feast of harvest a multitude of three thousand souls was gathered in, symbolizing the vast humanity to be brought into the church of God in the long remainder of the last days.

On Pentecost, therefore, the ascended Lord in the power of the Holy Spirit began the re-universalization of the redemptive work of God, for it was then that the church, the body of Christ, was born. The *ekklesia* of the New Testament replaced the *qahal* (congregation) of Israel, ecumenical Christianity replaced the Jewish national faith, proclamation and sacrament replaced sacrificial offering, the preacher replaced the priest, the communion table replaced the altar, baptism replaced circumcision; and everywhere believers called on God, worshiping not in the rituals of synagogue and temple, but in spirit and in truth.

In a traditional context, the idea of the inception of faith presented in this chapter raises a crucial question: how is the universal ability to believe the gospel related to God's sovereignty in Man's salvation? Is the certainty of salvation that is guaranteed by election to be exchanged for a universal ability to believe the gospel which a hearer may choose to exercise or not? Has God abdicated to the frailty of his fallen creature his power to save? To this question we turn in the next chapter.

Chapter VI

Salvation by Grace Alone

For by grace you have been saved through faith; and this is not your own doing, it is the gift of God.

Ephesians 2:8

When I say that "Man as *imago Dei* has the spiritual competence to respond affirmatively to the proclamation of the gospel," that he can "decide to believe the gospel" and can even "get" himself a new heart, that is, be born again, I mean in no way to affirm that he has this power "of himself" or "in himself," without enablement from God. Similarly, when I speak of "a salvation already achieved," I do not mean to affirm that this salvation is a static entity waiting to be "recognized and embraced."

The salvation which God has prepared in the incarnation, life, death, resurrection, ascension, and universal reign of our Lord is a dynamic force because it exists in the power of the outpoured Holy Spirit. It is God on the move to reclaim lost territory. It is announcement, with a voice that will not be silenced, that victory has been achieved over sin and death and the grave. This message-in-power from the Redeemer God blows on the glowing ember that is the Creator's remnant image-outpost in the dominion of darkness. There the "smoking flax" is fanned to flame by the congenial breath of the Redeemer Spirit and in its resuscitation is delivered from the confinement and restraint of sin to a life of service in the kingdom of God.

Because it *exists* and *lives,* this remaining image can respond to the dynamic proclamation with "I believe; help my unbelief!" (Mark 9:24). This capacity for response to the Redeemer God is the universal endowment of every human being, because all have been created in the image of God; and that image, though fallen, remains the image of God and is therefore never without the life of God in some degree. In the human soul the Redeemer God meets the Creator God and returns to him his lost dominion: "this my son was dead, and is alive again; he was lost, and is found" (Luke 15:24). Just as they began to make merry on earth (v. 24b), so there is joy in heaven among the angels of God over a sinner who repents (v. 10).

In the gospel as understood in historic Reformed teaching, there is an identical dynamism, but with this fateful qualification: the Redeemer God can address the sinner with the effect of repentance and faith in his life *only* if the sinner is elect. By a divine act of regeneration prior to or simultaneous with the proclamation, the hearer must be made receptive to the gospel. Only *then* can he believe, and only *such* can believe. The power of the Holy Spirit working in the witness of the proclamation cannot effect a new heart without the prior or concurrent special, individual divine gift of elective rebirth. Without this effective preparation to believe the gospel, the hearer cannot will to do the will of God (John 7:17), which is the conversion of every elect person who hears the gospel. Man dead in sins and trespasses does not have it "in himself" or "of himself" to believe the gospel and thus return to God. We must examine this proposition that no one has it "in himself" or "of herself" to believe the gospel when he or she hears it.

One would be reluctant to deny that anyone has it in himself to breathe or to walk or to see. We are endowed with many gifts of body, mind, and spirit which are natural to us, which belong to us "natively." It is when we abuse our ownership of these gifts that questions arise and judgment comes down—as instanced by Jesus in the parable of the rich fool, who said to his soul, "Soul, you have ample goods laid up for many years," and that very day his soul was called to account (Luke 12:19-20). More sophisticated fools pride themselves on their knowledge or skill or wisdom or high achievement.

In this discussion we are thinking of endowments that are properly stewarded and may therefore legitimately be said to be "mine" or "yours" or "theirs." Whatever a human being may legitimately be said to "have" does not, in the Reformed view, include the possibility of appropriating by faith the reconciliation between God and Man that has been wrought by Christ and made effective in life by the work of the Holy Spirit. The most devout cultivation of Man's inborn *sensus divinitatis* cannot enable one who is not numbered among the elect to believe the gospel. That can happen only as the result of a new birth, the bestowal of a gift of life arising exclusively out of election, which gift is called regeneration.

The unspoken assumption of the thesis that Man does not have it "of himself" or "in herself" to believe the gospel is that we do have some things "of ourselves." No one would quibble about the proposition that human beings are natively capable of breathing, walking, and seeing. But neither should anyone protest against the proposition that *everything* of which Man is "natively capable" is a gift of God. Of nothing is Man more capable than having good health; yet nothing so quickly brings us to the realization that health is a gift as a dose of serious illness. We must take with utter seriousness Paul's pertinent question to the Corinthian Christians, "What have you that you did not receive?" and the further supporting question, "If then you received it, why do you boast as if it were not a gift?" (1 Cor. 4:7). So, then, whatever we have is gifted to us by God, and to be gifted by God means to be a recipient of his goodness. It means the denial of the claim to autonomous existence.

The unconditionality of this truth is patent. Surely nothing in all the world is so much our own as our bodies. That is where all private right begins. But what is more obvious than their giftedness? Through conception and womb Man is brought forth. And that which is brought forth is altogether complete. The physically strongest, the athletically most agile, have added not a single component to their bodily structure. What they have done is to cultivate their health and develop the muscular and nervous potentials that resided natively within them beforehand.

It may be argued that this development is due to their own exertion and achievement. But with what right? As image of God, Man was created to be creative. Body is guided by mind and spirit. By means of these we have the power of reflection, of planning, of innovation, of strengthening will and motivation. The artist's perception of form, the musician's sensitivity to the harmony of sounds, the mathematician's feeling for numerical relations and exactitude—these and all other competencies are only the fruit of creationally willed and creationally bestowed potentials, aptitudes, instincts, and genius with which all members of the race are variously endowed.

If these endowments could be developed but are not, their recipients can fall under blame; if they are developed by imagination and exertion, the result may give satisfaction and evoke justifiable pride of achievement, but never a sense of being the unaided, self-determined creator of it. For every ingredient that goes into achievement is gifted, not least the potent intangibles of intuitive perception, willpower, and intellectual acuteness that stand at the center of every human undertaking. Not only in the spiritual but also in the natural realm, "it is God who works in you both to will and to act according to his good purpose" (Phil. 2:13); and again, "apart from me you can do nothing" (John 15:5).

The fact of the matter is that Man "of himself" has *absolutely nothing*—except sin, which is our own "creation." Man came forth out of nothing that was his, and if the grave is "nothing," then to nothing he returns. Job was correct: "Naked I came from my mother's womb, and naked shall I return; the Lord gave, and the Lord has taken away; blessed be the name of the Lord" (1:21). All things are from God, all things are from God only, and all that lies between divine creation and return to God has being and meaning only in relation to the Creator. To see that all "being" outside of this relationship is in fact nonbeing and to praise God that this is so because in him alone we live and move and have our being—this is the highest knowledge and true wisdom.

Therefore no one ever "has" anything in the sense in which secular Man considers himself to be the owner of his life, his strength, his competencies, and his earthly habitat. Mankind is indeed wealthy beyond any description. But all his wealth, all that he is and has, and all that he can become is gift, not property. Whatever he has is a stewardship, an entrustment, for the discharge of which he will be called to account. In Man's relationship to God, all that is horizontally owned is vertically held in trust; and this holding in trust for God determines how we exercise our stewardship in society.

If, then, God has been pleased to leave to fallen Man such a measure of his image as to retain for him the status of *imago Dei* and if in that status he responds believingly to the gospel, he is not doing this "of himself" or by means of anything that he has "in himself." He believes because he has been addressed by the gospel and has responded to that address by means of the given but dulled light of the *imago Dei,* which was fanned into flame within him by the power of the Spirit speaking the word of address. No one who knows himself to have been brought to Christ in that way can possibly vaunt himself, realizing that both the content of the message believed and the manner in which it was apprehended and appropriated are from God alone.

The essential difference between this exposition of how faith comes into being and the traditional Reformed conception centers on the role played by Man as *imago Dei.* According to the presentation here set forth, there is in all men natively—that is, as an essential part of their humanity—a point of contact on which the proclamation of the gospel can effectively impinge, in the sense that all men have within themselves the capacity of responding to it in true faith. That point of contact is the fundamental character of their being as image of God.

In the traditional Reformed understanding there is no assured point of contact in Man for the gospel to impact on. Before this can take place, it must first be created in him. It is called the new birth or regeneration, and it takes place only in those who have been elected or ordained to receive it according to God's eternal decree. In the thesis here propounded, the addressee can yield to the effectuating Spirit; he can also resist and reject him. In the Reformed view the Holy Spirit is the effectuating agent whose irresistible grace cannot be rejected. Infallibly he brings all the elect to faith, to salvation, and to eternal bliss, from which all not electively endowed with his grace are irrevocably excluded.

For a long time Reformed theology retained its place in the theological spectrum because of the compelling logical deductions it made from the basic premise of the sovereignty of God. This divine supremacy was thought to center in an inscrutable exercise of divine will as "sovereign good pleasure," and this good pleasure it was neither permissible nor possible to analyze or to explore. Presumably for this reason the tragic fate of the reprobate was never dwelt upon. But the comfort given to true believers by the certainty of election was often counterbalanced in the less assured by the horrible contemplation that they might be reprobate and therefore deprived by divine *fiat* of all hope in this life and in the life to come. And in spite of remonstrances and denials, the crafting of the doctrines of election and reprobation in theology and creed never succeeded wholly in freeing God from the suspicion that somehow or other he had no small hand in effecting the ultimate woe as well as the ultimate weal of men.

In the end, the cornerstone doctrine of predestination became a victim of erosion that could not be stayed. Several factors wore it down. There was, first, the simple reading of the Scriptures, which does not encourage the sophistication demanded by the refined but unconvincing distinctions of Reformed predestination theology. In the second place, continuing criticism of the exegetical basis for reprobation both outside of and within the Reformed community had its effect. Thirdly, the pastoral infelicity of the use of the doctrine of reprobation in the pulpit and the absurdity of its use on the mission field forced it more and more to the periphery of theological and churchly interest. In consequence, there developed in the Reformed and Presbyterian churches the realization that a Christianity defined in terms of traditional Reformed predestination theology cannot remain viable.

It is the duty of the theological community to take seriously the systematic articulation of the teaching of Scripture on so fundamental a doctrine as the source and manner of the rise of saving faith in the hearts of people. The Reformed community is called to live theologically as well as ecclesiastically by the watchword of the Reformation: *semper reformanda,* "ever reforming." It would seem that conceptions of the role played by Man as *imago Dei,* the power of the Holy Spirit in the renewal of Man as *imago Dei,* and the universalism of God's grace should form significant components in the restructuring of historic Reformed theological thought.

The question will naturally be asked how the proclamation of the gospel can affect people so variously? Some hear it and immediately believe, only to fall away after a time; some who believe remain staunch in the faith. Still others hear it, are indifferent, but yield to its power in the end. In some human areas the gospel is more readily received than in others, and rootage in depth lends firmness and strength to the faith. In the twentieth century the gospel spread phenomenally among the peoples of Africa south of the Sahara, while vast missionary efforts in India, China, and southeast Asia over a longer time have been far less fruitful. In the Western countries the secular spirit has during the present century taken a very great toll in membership and Christian commitment in the mainline churches, but this is being counteracted by an evangelical resurgence through new and less structured communions.

Persuasive historical, cultural, and religious reasons can be adduced to explain Christian increase and decrease in various regions and historical periods, and it is wise to take these into careful account. But considerations that shed light on the progress of the gospel in one area often fail wholly to explain the lack of success in another where the known forces at work were very similar. The categories of election and reprobation may satisfy the traditional Reformed mind in personal individual cases, but it is wholly baffled by the complexities of peoples' movements toward Christianity and by the broad and varying tides of secular and church history.

It is precisely at this point that the concept of the image of God becomes helpful in assessing the general as well as the local and individual Christian situation. Constant amid all the turmoil of history is the fact that every human being has the capacity for faith in Christ. There is no question here of a secret divine decree destining some for salvation and others for perdition. However laden with consequence in eternity faith and unbelief may be, they are not grounded in a pre-creational divine decree. Both take their rise in time. Whoever hears the gospel is, because of his sinful nature, disposed to reject it, but because of the light and life vouchsafed to him as participating in the *imago Dei,* he is also capable of believing it. The intent of the witnessing Spirit is the same for all—it is salvation.

We saw in the previous chapter that this is made very clear and explicit in Canons of Dort III-IV.8: "As many as are called by the gospel are unfeignedly called. For God has most earnestly and truly declared in his Word what is acceptable to him, namely, that those who are called should come to him. He also seriously promises rest of soul and eternal life to all who come to him and believe." How the reprobating God of Canons of Dort I.6 and I.15 can "unfeignedly" call those to him in time concerning whom he has in eternity decreed "not to bestow on them saving faith and the grace of conversion" is a mystery on which Reformed theology sheds no light. The more is the contradiction complete in that III-IV.9 makes it indisputably clear that by "call" in Article 8 is meant not the internal calling that is inseparable from elect regeneration but the universally extended call that impinges on the ear of the hearer.

When we speak ironically in this connection of a "mystery" in Reformed theology, it is not to suggest that the present exposition ignores the reality of mystery in the saving work of God. On the contrary, it is most emphatically affirmed. The "mystery" that confronts us in the Canons of Dort in the decree of reprobation (I.6, 15) on the one hand and the "unfeigned" universal call to faith and salvation (III-IV.8) on the other is in fact not a mystery, but a plain contradiction and therefore an irrationality.

The true mystery at the heart of both creation and redemption is grounded in the fact that each is a work of God, who, because he is wholly Logos, cannot be fully comprehended by his created human image. It is of this kind of mystery that we must further speak as we try to understand the relationship between faith and Man's being as *imago Dei.*

There are in the Bible allusions and references to mystery that, far from being enigmatic or forbidding, gently invite exploration. One of the authors of Proverbs writes,

> Three things are too wonderful for me;
> four I do not understand:
> the way of an eagle in the sky,
> the way of a serpent on a rock,
> the way of a ship on the high seas,
> and the way of a man with a maiden. (30:18-19)

Here are the wonder, admiration, and curiosity that form the beginning of all inquiry and understanding. In Psalm 139:1-6 the poet marvels at God's knowledge of him: "Thou searchest out my path and my lying down, and art acquainted with all my ways. . . . Such knowledge is too wonderful for me; . . . I cannot attain it." God's knowledge of us transcends our self-knowledge, but the poet knows this only because of his self-examination; the more deeply he pursues it, the more he wonders at the depth and magnitude of the divine knowledge. According to 1 Peter 1:10-12, the prophets "searched and inquired" what person or time was indicated by the Spirit when he predicted the suffering of Christ and the subsequent glory. But what was mysterious to them has now been openly announced in the gospel, while yet the mystery remains for the angels, who long to look into these revelations.

Profoundest of all, however, are St. Paul's references to divine mystery. His use of this concept must be distinguished from our common understanding of the "mysterious" as unknown. The mystery of which Paul speaks is a *known* mystery. God has "made known" to the church "the mystery of his will" (Eph. 1:9). Paul has been given "insight into the mystery of Christ" (3:4); he tells the church a mystery: "We shall not all sleep, but we shall all be changed" (1 Cor. 15:51). The mystery that has been hidden for ages and generations is now "made manifest to his saints," the mystery "which is Christ in you, the hope of glory" (Col. 1:26-27). So the mystery is open, not a secret matter known only to God. It is a revelation that must be explored in order to be understood, made known, and transmitted to succeeding generations. The more knowledge and understanding of it grow, the more the wonder, the marvel, the glory, the profundity of it increase. The mystery of salvation is very like the mystery of creation in macrocosm and microcosm—the farther the telescope probes the heavens and the microscope plumbs the invisible world of infinitesimally minute organic and inorganic matter, the more we discover new worlds to be explored and the more we understand that God alone is great.

In all these things, the words of Moses remain true, "The secret things belong to the Lord our God; but the things that are revealed belong to us and to our children for ever, that we may do all the words of this law" (Deut. 29:29). The origin of unbelief in human life, according to the consistent witness of Scripture, lies in Man, not in God. How sin and evil could arise in a world made "very good" by the holy Creator is an impenetrable mystery. It has been called "the impossible possibility": impossible because it could not happen, possible because it did. The Scriptures recognize the reality of sin and death, but nowhere do they explain these phenomena. This recognition is a powerful acknowledgment, however, for it is concretized in the uncompromising divine war on and total conquest of sin, death, and the grave and in the reconstitution of the universe in a state of goodness that can never again be betrayed.

A striking aspect of God's attitude to evil is the pervasive scriptural thrust of the surprise of God and of his spokesmen at the existence of unbelief. One marvels at the mildness of God's rebuke of Man's first sin: "Who told you that you were naked? Have you eaten of the tree of which I commanded you not to eat?" (Gen. 3:11). But the depth of the divine incredulity that such a thing could happen may be measured by Adam's and Eve's consternation and their hiding themselves among the trees of the garden from the presence and the wrath of God, and their expulsion from its felicity (Gen. 3:6-24). Through Isaiah God complains, "The ox knows its owner, and the ass its master's crib; but Israel does not know, my people does not understand" (1:3); and again, "O inhabitants of Jerusalem and men of Judah, judge, I pray you, between me and my vineyard. What more was there to do for my vineyard, that I have not done in it? When I looked for it to yield grapes, why did it yield wild grapes?" (5:3-4). Through Micah he pleads, "O my people, what have I done to you? In what have I wearied you? Answer me!" (6:3).

In Matthew 23:37 Jesus exclaims, "O Jerusalem, Jerusalem, . . . How often would I have gathered your children together as a hen gathers her brood under her wings, and you would not!" Mark reports that in his own Galilean homeland Jesus "could do no mighty work there, except that he laid his hands upon a few sick people and healed them. And he marveled because of their unbelief" (6:5-6). In John 3:10-11 Jesus rebukes Nicodemus, "Are you a teacher of Israel, and yet you do not understand this? Truly, truly, I say to you, we speak of what we know, and bear witness to what we have seen; but you do not receive our testimony." And in 12:37 John sadly reports, "Though he had done so many signs before them, yet they did not believe in him." To the Galatian Christians Paul writes, "I am astonished that you are so quickly deserting him who called you in the grace of Christ and turning to a different gospel" (1:6).

In short, there is mystery in the realm of sin as there is mystery in the realm of grace. In 2 Thessalonians 2:3-12 St. Paul even speaks explicitly of "the mystery of lawlessness" (v. 7), which is intimately related to "the man of lawlessness, . . . the son of perdition" (v. 3b), who will appear and be destroyed in his time. And there is "the mystery of the woman and the beast" described in Revelation 17:1-8. The wholly opposite dimensions of sin and grace, which constitute the poles between which the drama of salvation moves, are permeated by ultimate incomprehensibility and unfathomableness.

But there is a notable difference. The Scriptures treat sin and death as stark and terrible mysteries which have in principle been conquered and put away by the work of Christ. They are therefore not subjects that have an inherent attractiveness. They are not a revelation of God's being and work. The Bible exposes them for what they are but has no independent interest in them. On the other hand, Scripture treats nature and grace as powers of infinite beauty and loveliness which invite ever deepening admiration and appropriation to the glory of God, who is their overflowing source.

Against this background we must now inquire more particularly into the mystery of the relationship between faith in Christ as a universal human possibility and sinful man as *imago Dei* who is called to have that faith. We shall examine it in terms of a well-known conversation between Jesus and the Pharisee Nicodemus. The conversation in full reads as follows:

> Now there was a man of the Pharisees, named Nicodemus, a ruler of the Jews. This man came to Jesus by night and said to him, "Rabbi, we know that you are a teacher come from God; for no one can do these signs that you do, unless God is with him." Jesus answered him, "Truly, truly, I say to you, unless one is born anew, he cannot see the kingdom of God." Nicodemus said to him, "How can a man be born when he is old? Can he enter a second time into his mother's womb and be born?" Jesus answered, "Truly, truly, I say to you, unless one is born of water and the Spirit, he cannot enter the kingdom of God. That which is born of the flesh is flesh, and that which is born of the Spirit is spirit. Do not marvel that I

said to you, 'You must be born anew.' The wind blows where it wills, and you hear the sound of it, but you do not know whence it comes or whither it goes; so it is with every one who is born of the Spirit." Nicodemus said to him, "How can this be?" Jesus answered him, "Are you a teacher of Israel, and yet you do not understand this? Truly, truly, I say to you, we speak of what we know, and bear witness to what we have seen; but you do not receive our testimony. If I have told you earthly things and you do not believe, how can you believe if I tell you heavenly things? No one has ascended into heaven but he who descended from heaven, the Son of man. And as Moses lifted up the serpent in the wilderness, so must the Son of man be lifted up, that whoever believes in him may have eternal life." (John 3:1-15)

It seems at first glance that we must choose here between two irreconcilable statements. In verse 3 Jesus says, "unless one is born anew [or from above], he cannot see the kingdom of God"; verses 14-15 say that as Moses lifted up the serpent in the wilderness, so must the Son of man be lifted up "that whoever believes in him may have eternal life." In verse 3, being born from above seems to be the condition for believing, as indeed it is in traditional Reformed theology. In verse 15, there appears to be no condition at all for faith. Simply believe, and you will have eternal life.

This understanding receives support in Numbers 21:9, to which Jesus alludes. As the people of Israel who had been struck by venomous serpents could be healed simply by looking at the figure of a bronze serpent that Moses had displayed, so "whoever believes" in the Son of Man may have eternal life. Here there is no question of prior condition: the words "and if a serpent bit any man, he would look at the bronze serpent and live" seem to find their equivalent in Jesus' words, "whoever believes in him [the Son] may have eternal life."

There is, however, a third declaration by Jesus in this passage, which removes the either-or character of the two statements we have quoted. To Nicodemus's question, "Can he enter a second time into his mother's womb and be born?" Jesus answered, "Truly, truly, I say to you, unless one is born of water and the

Spirit, he cannot enter the kingdom of God" (v. 5). In this response there is a double condition for entering God's kingdom. It constitutes a fusion of new birth (v. 3) and believing (v. 15) into one indivisible happening—birth through baptism and birth through the Holy Spirit. But what is baptism? Is it not the sacramental seal of God upon the hearing and believing of the gospel? Mark 16:15-16—though the authenticity of the text is questioned—includes the thoroughly scriptural coordination of preaching, faith, and baptism: "Go into all the world and preach the gospel to the whole creation. He who believes and is baptized will be saved."[1] And as baptism is inseparable from hearing the Word of God, so the work of the Spirit is inseparable from believing that Word. That is to say, the faith of the believer and the new birth that underlies and informs it constitute an intertwining, indivisible, and as such a basically unitary divine-human transaction.

In his Anchor Bible commentary on John, Raymond E. Brown puts the matter succinctly: "If we take vs. 5 as a reference to Baptism and faith, then begetting of water and Spirit are two co-ordinate exigencies for entering the kingdom of God."[2] The Spirit of God the Redeemer coming "from above" speaks to the muted Spirit of the Creator in the fallen *imago* of the addressed person, fans its embers into flame, is met with the response of faith, and thus brings into being the new man in Christ in the ineffable mystery of divine-human conjunction. This is regeneration; this is the new birth; this is conversion.

In the face of the apostolic "What have you that you did not receive?" (1 Cor. 4:7), the question of what is of God and what is of Man is utterly irrelevant here. It is *in God* that we live and move and have our being, but it is in God that *we* live, and *we* move, and *we* have *our* being. Our living, our moving, our being are real and true; and they are never to be discounted, for they

1. Cf. Matt. 28:19; Acts 2:38-41, 8:12, 8:35-38, 10:44-48, 19:1-5; Gal. 3:25-27; Eph. 4:1-6; Col. 2:12.

2. Raymond E. Brown, *The Gospel According to John (i-xii),* Anchor Bible Series Vol. 29 (Garden City, NY: Doubleday, 1966), p. 144.

are all exercised in God. He is not pleased by our diminishing that aspect of his image which is essential to its integrity, that is, the gift of full responsibility, specifically the gift of responding to divine address. In his response to Nicodemus, Jesus stresses this. "Truly, truly, I say to you, we speak of what we know, and bear witness to what we have seen; *but you do not receive our testimony.*" God is pleased when the unbelieving believe, when those not reciprocating his trust return it, when the disobedient obey. In such belief, such trust, such obedience he finds himself reflected, for in the sacred trinity there is ever the response of love to love. We may not fail to mention here those of the human family who do not have the gift of full responsibility, such as children who die before reaching the age of spiritual discretion and those who because of deficient natural endowment are unable to respond. They too have a Father in heaven who knows and understands them.

At every point where divine and human, infinity and finitude, eternity and time effect a conjunction, there is mystery. In theology this mystery comes to particular expression in the union of the divine and the human. How could God become man? What is the relationship between the divine and the human in Christ? It is thus inevitable that mystery should surround Man as the finite image of the eternal God, particularly when the horizontal line of his life on earth is intersected by the vertical line come down from heaven. The Nicodemus passage significantly emphasizes the mystery on the human as well as on the divine side which attends the saving work of the Holy Spirit. In commenting on his own words "You must be born anew," Jesus said, "The wind blows where it wills, and you hear the sound of it, but you do not know whence it comes or whither it goes; so it is with every one who is born of the Spirit" (vv. 7-8). Thus the mystery is as great in the recipient of gracc as it is in its Bestower. As such it invites exploration as well as admiration, reverence, and worship, but always in the realization that we explore, admire, and revere *mystery,* which in its depth, breadth, and height evokes worship and adoration of God, who dwells in light unapproachable, the light that reveals what can be apprehended but not comprehended.

At this point, too, Brown is helpful:

> Although we can see the effects of *pneuma* (wind) all about us, no one can actually see the *pneuma* (wind) that causes these effects. So too one can see those who are begotten from above through *pneuma* (Spirit), those who have accepted Jesus, without seeing just when or how this *pneuma* (Spirit) begets them, and without knowing why one man accepts Jesus and another does not.[3]

With the element of mystery in the saving work of God, particularly in the regeneration of the human heart, Reformed theology heartily concurs. But there is one aspect of the mystery affirmed in the present book which the Reformed tradition wholly disowns. It rejects completely Brown's final words: "without knowing why one man accepts Jesus and another does not." Reformed theology knows *precisely* why "one man accepts Jesus and another does not." Only the elect believe, only the elect *can* believe, and without fail all the elect *will* believe. The constraint of the Spirit is not external—it is organic; it is free, involving intellect, feeling, and will—but it is certain and definite and inevitable. The reprobate, on the other hand, *cannot* believe, for they are left in their sin by God and are ordained by him never to see the light of life.

Chapter III of the Westminster Confession of Faith of 1643 is as unambiguous on this point as the Canons of Dort:

> By the decree of God, for the manifestation of his glory, some men and angels are predestined to everlasting life, and others foreordained to everlasting death.
>
> These . . . are particularly and unchangeably designed; and their number is so certain and definite that it cannot be either increased or diminished. . . .

3. Brown, p. 141.

> Wherefore they who are elected being fallen in Adam, are redeemed by Christ. . . . Neither are any other redeemed by Christ . . . but the elect only.
>
> The rest of mankind, God was pleased . . . to pass by, and to ordain them to dishonour and wrath for their sin, to the praise of his glorious justice. (III.3-4, 6-7)

Although this position has now been widely given up by the Presbyterian and Reformed churches worldwide, an undeniable ambiguity remains in the resulting understanding. Reprobation has been repudiated not so much by credal or even theological revision as by being ignored or silenced to death. But to repudiate reprobation while retaining a numerical conception of election leaves wide open the problem of the "non-elect."

For now, I shall leave this question and, in closing this chapter, point to an aspect of the scriptural teaching of salvation by grace alone which seems to me to be too often overlooked: the element of doxology. A doxology is an attribution of praise to God. Three examples follow:

> O the depth of the riches and wisdom and knowledge of God! How unsearchable are his judgments and how inscrutable his ways!
>
> "For who has known the mind of the Lord,
> or who has been his counselor?" . . .
>
> For from him and through him and to him are all things. To him be glory for ever. Amen. (Rom. 11:33-36)

An innumerable multitude from all nations, tribes, and peoples stood before the throne of God and before the Lamb and cried out with a mighty voice, "Salvation belongs to our God who sits upon the throne, and to the Lamb!" And all the angels standing around the throne and round the elders and the four living creatures fell on their faces and worshiped God, saying "Amen! Blessing and glory and wisdom and thanksgiving and honor and power and might be to our God for ever and ever!" (Rev. 7:9-12).

Then John heard what seemed to be the voice of a great multitude, like the sound of many waters, crying,

> "Hallelujah! For the Lord our God the Almighty reigns.
> Let us rejoice and exult and give him the glory,
> for the marriage of the Lamb has come,
> and his Bride has made herself ready;
> it was granted her to be clothed in fine linen, bright and pure."
> (Rev. 19:6-8)

While God's people are in the present dispensation, they lead a varied life, and much depends on the way in which they handle themselves. There is much for them to do that is difficult and much to refrain from doing which is often no less difficult. Tasks are assigned; there is joy in the work; there are disappointments and weariness. There are encouragements and discouragements. There are achievements and there are failures. There is praise and there is blame.

When we read the doxologies we find none of these things—neither the good nor the bad, neither the successes nor the failures are recounted. There is only God, and he is all and in all. To him is the last word because from him was the first word. From him, through him, and to him are all things.

As we struggle through our history, managing our talents as we are able, doing despite our shortcomings much that receives commendation on earth and praise in heaven, we find at last that all our competence, all our vision, all our achieving were from God alone and that to him belong the praise and the honor and the glory.

Salvation belongs to God, for by grace we are being saved through faith, and this is not our own doing; it is the gift of God. Yet in the allness of God's salvation there is the indispensable component called faith, which is *our* faith, not *his* faith, however much it is his *gift.*

And who is sufficient for these things? (2 Cor. 2:16).

Chapter VII

Those Who Did Not Hear the Gospel

Truly I perceive that God shows no partiality, but in every nation any one who fears him and does what is right is acceptable to him.

Acts 10:34-35

At a conference of the Fellowship of Christian Students in Northern Nigeria in the 1960s, I shared a room with a leader in one of Northern Nigeria's largest denominations. Toward the end of the conference, when we had gotten to know each other a bit, he unburdened himself about a problem that weighed heavily on his heart.

"You know," he said, "that we Africans hold our ancestors in high regard. When we become Christians, we do not cease to keep them in our affection and respect. But the mission that brought my church into being believes that all ancestors who never heard the gospel are forever lost. They did not know the Lord Jesus Christ and therefore have passed into a Christless eternity. This teaching bothers me deeply. We owe our tribal existence, our culture, our language, our traditions to our ancestors. That we Christians shall be forever separated from them is a hard teaching."

His concern was not new to me. No one can be missionarily alert in Africa south of the Sahara and remain unaware of the place that the ancestors occupy in the African mind. In their own way, all Africans consider themselves to be surrounded by a "cloud of witnesses," invisible to the eye but very real. They are "the living dead," and this belief profoundly influences the living. At the same time, the gospel is for the living, and it is not difficult to see that a simplistic conception of it could lead to the conclusion that my companion so deeply deplored and questioned. Moreover, his concern arose not only from his tribal tradition but also from a sense of equity and fairness in God which the gospel itself had nurtured in him.

It was at this point of fairness that we found common ground. I recalled the familiar story of Genesis 18, which recounts the Lord's visit to Abraham with two angel companions. Having refreshed them, Abraham accompanied the Lord for a distance and learned the purpose of his journey. The outcry against the evil of the cities of Sodom and Gomorrah was so great that God had decided to investigate whether all he had heard was true. Sensing what this meant, Abraham, whose nephew Lot lived in Sodom, began the famous bargaining encounter with the Lord. Would God indeed destroy the righteous with the wicked? Would the Judge of all the earth not do right? Suppose there were fifty righteous in the city, or forty-five, or thirty, or twenty, or ten? Each time the Lord yielded. Underlying the whole intercession of Abraham was this basic principle: shall not the Judge of all the earth do right?

If then, in our opinion, it is a matter of fairness that the ancestors who never heard the gospel be not eternally separated from their posterity who heard and accepted it, should we not believe that God's sense of fairness and equity is as great as our own? Is it not in fact far greater? Can he not make the life, death, and resurrection of Christ efficacious backward as well as forward? Was the pious Israelite before Christ not saved by the same Lord as we are? Did Jesus not die for all mankind?

I asked my brother in Christ, "Are you able to leave your

problem in the hand of that Lord, who is as loving as he is just and as just as he is loving?"

He looked at me for a long moment; then he said, "If only my missionaries would say that, I would be satisfied."

Put in terms of our discussion in this book, the question that troubled this African Christian is this: what is the significance of mankind as the image of God for the relationship to God of those who have never heard the gospel? Are they destined to remain forever "separated from Christ . . . having no hope and without God in the world" (Eph. 2:12)?

We may begin by looking at some key passages in which Herman Bavinck deals with the relationship between general revelation and the ethnic religions:

> It is true that the Bible judges severely the character of the ethnic religions; it is no less true that the general revelation which the Scriptures themselves teach gives us the right to acknowledge all the elements of truth which are present in them. The study of the world's religions was in earlier times dominated by dogmatic and apologetic theology. Founders of religions, such as Muhammad, were simply regarded as deceivers, enemies of God, minions of the devil. Since we have come to know these religions more accurately, this understanding has become untenable; it stands in conflict with both history and psychology.
>
> According to the Scriptures there is also among non-Christian peoples a revelation of God, an enlightenment by the Logos, a working of God's Spirit. . . . Augustine could speak unfavorably about the Gentiles, but nevertheless acknowledges that they saw the truth in shadowy form, that it was not altogether hidden from them, and that we should therefore appropriate whatever is true in their philosophy. . . .
>
> Not only in science and art . . . but also in the ethnic religions we see a working of God's Spirit. . . . For the founders of these religions . . . were men who were religiously disposed, imbued with a calling to fulfill, frequently influencing men beneficently. . . . Not only cries of despair but also declarations of confidence, hope, serenity, peace . . . meet us in the pagan world. All the elements and forms essential to religion are present in them: a God-concept,

a sense of guilt, need for salvation, sacrifice, priesthood, temple, worship and prayer exist in marred but living form in the ethnic religions. Even unconscious prophecies and striking expectations of a better and purer religion are not wanting.

Therefore Christianity does not stand exclusively over against them; it is also the fulfillment of the ethnic religions. . . . What is appearance there is reality here; what is sought there is found here; Christianity is the explanation of the problem of ethnic religions. Christ is the one promised to Israel, he is the desire of all nations, Israel and the church are elect for the sake of mankind. In Abraham's seed all the generations of the earth are blessed. . . .

Moreover, in that general revelation [out of which the ethnic religions arose] the believer finds a firm ground on which he can meet all who are not Christian. He has a common foundation with them. His Christian faith may press him into a position of isolation; he may not be able to prove the validity of his religious convictions to others. Nevertheless, in general revelation he has a point of contact with all who bear the name of Man.

The error of supposing that natural religion and natural theology have an independent existence in no wise changes the fact that from within creation, from nature and history, from heart and conscience, a speech of God comes to every human being. No one escapes the power of God's general revelation. Religion belongs to the very being of Man. The idea of God and the existence of God, the spiritual reality and eternal destiny of Man, origin and rationale of creation, the moral world order and its ultimate triumph—all are problems that give no rest to the human spirit.

The claims of these profound demands do not permit themselves to be suppressed. Philosophy does not cease its efforts to deal with and satisfy them. It is general revelation that keeps this need alive. It prevents Man from sinking to the animal level. It binds him to the supersensible world. It maintains in him the realization that he has been created in the image of God and finds no other rest in the world than in God alone.

General revelation preserves humanity in order that it may be found by Christ and restored to its rightful mind. To that extent natural theology was in early times called a preamble to faith, a divine preparation and tutelage for Christianity. General revelation is the foundation on which special revelation stands and speaks.[1]

Bavinck seems to put the ethnic religions in a sort of religious twilight zone—neither in fellowship with God nor yet out of touch with him, a "court of the Gentiles" within the "temple area" but outside the temple's blessing. He sees this humanity as consisting of addressable persons who have within themselves a point of contact that gives common ground to Christian and non-Christian. It is this quality we have spoken about in the present book as the residual *imago Dei.* By reason of it all men have a sense of the divine and in one way or another express their innate religious bent. It is the capability that makes it possible for Man to react in some degree to God's revelation of himself in the natural world and to respond with faith to the message of the gospel when he hears it.

In this chapter we are concerned with Man's religious response to God's revelation of himself in nature. It deals with all that humanity which in the era before Christ was not of Israel and in the present era lives outside the hearing of the gospel. It includes all humanity that has never heard or has not yet heard the gospel, and secular Man, by which we mean that segment of humanity, predominantly in the once generally Christian West and belonging to the time commonly called post-Christian, for whom belief in the gospel is seen as a precluded option.

In seeking to understand the relationship of this humanity to God's general revelation, we should recognize the smallness of the Christian segment in relation to the whole of humanity today

1. Bavinck, *Gereformeerde Dogmatiek,* 1:330-35 passim. In his two-volume *Foundations of Dogmatics,* Otto Weber refers to Bavinck's magnum opus in a number of connections and describes it as "a comprehensive and still very usable dogmatics" (trans. Darrell L. Guder, vol. 1 [Grand Rapids: Eerdmans, 1981], p. 156 n. 88). In the judgment of the present writer, it would be difficult to find a more adequate theological statement of the Christian view of the ethnic religions in brief compass than is given in the unabbreviated form of the citation adduced here.

and, indeed, throughout history. Until the nineteenth century Christianity was largely confined to the West, meaning Europe and its extensions in Australia, New Zealand, South Africa, and the Americas. Moreover, it was almost wholly white in race. From the time of Abraham to the outpouring of the Holy Spirit on the day of Pentecost, God's redemptive revelation was confined to Israel, and even there it was more disregarded than believed.

In the nineteenth and twentieth centuries a worldwide missionary expansion of the faith took place, but this has been accompanied in the twentieth century by great losses to secularism in the West and by the suppression of the church by Communist states in large areas. Great gains were made, however, in the islands of Oceania, the Philippines, Korea, and especially Africa. But the vast human areas served by Islam, Hinduism, and Buddhism were touched only peripherally by the gospel or not at all.

The problem that confronts the thoughtful Christian is the nature of the relationship of the non-Christian world to God. And this non-Christian world includes that large segment of the so-called Christian world that is Christian in name but hardly distinguishable from secular humanity. The name "Christian" has for many come to be identified so much with being a good neighbor, a concerned citizen, a responsible parent, an honest and especially a likeable person, in short, a horizontally oriented human being, that the vertical dimension of the biblical sense of the word plays little or no role.

Whether secular or so-called Christian or religiously ethnic, all are consciously or unconsciously alien to the only name under heaven given among men whereby we must be saved (Acts 4:8-12; cf. 1 Cor. 2:2, 3:11). But if God does not wish that any should perish, but that all should reach repentance (2 Pet. 3:9), is it not equally true that his arm is not shortened so that it cannot save (Isa. 59:1)? Is there salvation only for those who have heard and believed and lived the gospel, with all others standing outside the embrace of God's saving love? Is Christ the expiation for the sins of believers only but not in fact "also for the sins of the whole world" (1 John 2:2)?

It would be a simple matter to resort at this point to a benign universal salvation, in which a final act of forgiveness and reconciliation resolved all the tensions between righteous God and unrepentant Man, between divine goodness and human evil, between heavenly wisdom and earthly folly. Isn't this, after all, the thing for a God of love to do? Should he "show his anger" forever? Did Christ not die for all? When we take the Bible seriously, such questions are frivolous and offensive, for Scripture speaks very plainly about judgment:

> For the time has come for judgment to begin with the household of God; and if it begins with us, what will be the end of those who do not obey the gospel of God? And
> "If the righteous man is scarcely saved,
> where will the impious and sinner appear?" (1 Pet. 4:17-18)

> For we must all appear before the judgment seat of Christ, so that each one may receive good or evil, according to what he has done in the body. (2 Cor. 5:10)

> [At the approach of the judgment] the kings of the earth and the great men and the generals and the rich and the strong, and every one, slave and free, hid in the caves and among the rocks of the mountains, calling to the mountains and rocks, "Fall on us and hide us from the face of him who is seated on the throne, and from the wrath of the Lamb, for the great day of their wrath has come, and who can stand before it?" (Rev. 6:15-16)

> Do not marvel at this; for the hour is coming when all who are in the tombs will hear his voice and come forth, those who have done good, to the resurrection of life, and those who have done evil, to the resurrection of judgment. (John 5:28-29)

> "Depart from me, you cursed, into the eternal fire prepared for the devil and his angels; for I was hungry and you gave me no food, I was thirsty and you gave me no drink. . . . Truly, I say to you, as you did it not to one of the least of these, you did it not to me." And they will go away into eternal punishment, but the righteous into eternal life. (Matt. 25:41, 45-46)

> Do not be deceived; God is not mocked, for whatever a man sows, that he will also reap. For he who sows to his own flesh will from the flesh reap corruption; but he who sows to the Spirit will from the Spirit reap eternal life. (Gal. 6:7-8)

The question is not whether there will or will not be a judgment. The history of nations and peoples, not least of Israel and the church, clamor for it insistently. Were there to be no final reckoning of accounts, God would not be God. But so much is he the upholder and vindicator of justice that judgment will begin "with the household of God" (1 Pet. 4:17). If it begins there, those who have spurned his house cannot complain when just sentence is pronounced against themselves. Amos disillusioned all who thought judgment was only for others: "Woe to you who desire the day of the Lord! Why would you have the day of the Lord? It is darkness, and not light. . . . Is not the day of the Lord darkness, and not light, and gloom with no brightness in it?" (5:18, 20). But for the afflicted and brokenhearted, "the day of vengeance of our God" will also "comfort all who mourn; . . . to give them a garland instead of ashes," so that God may be glorified (Isa. 61:2-3).

In the context of this chapter, therefore, the question is whether there will be vindication, justice, and reward also for the devotees of traditional religions and for all others who have not known or heard with understanding God's redemptive revelation. That is the question to which we now address ourselves.

We have noted the central role which Man as *imago Dei* plays in the hearing of the gospel. It is a role of response. God speaks the word of life and Man answers, either in faith or in unbelief, but he cannot fail to respond. The answer of faith is not possible, however, without the speaking of the Redeemer God in the power of the Holy Spirit. This fans into flame the light of the image of God within him and brings into being the new life in Christ. It is thus reasonable to assume that there is an activity of Man as *imago Dei* also in response to the speech of God the Creator in the natural world. That is to say, God's revelation in nature and in conscience as well as in grace is directed to Man as his image.

The fact that Man in his sin suppresses that revelation does not mean that he is not being addressed by it. The act of revealing implies not only a revealer but also a recipient. Revelation involves at the very least *intended* reception. God does not reveal himself to the oceans or the mountains or the prairie, nor to birds and animals and fish and insects. That would mean only that God reveals himself to his revelation. These are precisely the *vestigia Dei* that constitute his revelation.

God reveals himself in his creation to the climactic aspect of his self-revelation, which is *both* revelation *and* recipient, namely the creature called Man. In the creation of Man God mirrors himself back to himself; in that same creative act he reveals himself to his *imago.* Man in his quality and capacity as image of God is by that fact *homo sapiens,* who studies created reality and finds God's power and wisdom in all that he sees, not least in the nature and structure of his own being.

Because Man has been made in the image of God, he intuits God in his works. His very creation constituted him with the faculty of knowing God directly without having to resort to processes of rational thought and inference, though these doubtless amplify his intuition. It is doubtless this intuition that Paul has in mind when he writes, "For what can be known about God is plain to them, because God has shown it to them. Ever since the creation of the world his invisible nature, namely, his eternal power and deity, has been clearly perceived in the things that have been made" (Rom. 1:19-20). This revelation was the primordial, fundamental, adequate, and enduring self-manifestation of God. The image of God as living and organic being cannot fail to sense, within itself and in the larger creation of which it is both part and apex, the mighty Creator of all that is.

This inevitable and natural recognition and acceptance of God the Creator by Man the creature was so distorted by the fall into sin that from Man's side alienation from God took the place of fellowship and reciprocity. The revelation remained, loud and clear, both within him and around him, but he suppressed his perception of it. Unable to escape his being as creature and thereby his status of dependence on a power greater than himself, he indulged his flawed religious sensibilities and fashioned his own deities and the forms by which to worship them. Although men knew God, "they did not honor him as God or give thanks to him, but they became futile in their thinking and their senseless minds were darkened. Claiming to be wise, they became fools, and exchanged the glory of the immortal God for images resembling mortal man or birds or animals or reptiles" (Rom. 1:21-23).

Even so, as Bavinck points out, the religions of mankind formally manifest all the elements of true religion. Indeed, so related to true religious instincts were the outward forms of Semitic religion that Israel took over many of the external phenomena of its worship from the surrounding nations. What was lacking was orientation to the one and only God, who in the fullness of time came to his own world in the incarnate One, and it received him not (John 1:9-11). Therefore, says Paul, the Gentiles were "alienated from the commonwealth of Israel, and strangers to the covenants of promise, having no hope and without God in the world" (Eph. 2:12).

Yet such devastating words are by no means all that Scripture has to say about the Gentiles. Of all the parables of Jesus none is better known than that of the "Good Samaritan." Now the Samaritans were not precisely Gentiles, but neither were they considered to be Jews. The Samaritan religion was a mixture of Mosaic elements and Oriental beliefs introduced by people from such foreign places as Babylonia and Hamath whom the Assyrian conqueror Shalmaneser had settled in Samaria. An overlay of Yahwism covered a basically heathen religion. Thus Jesus could say to a Samaritan woman, "You worship what you do not know; we worship what we know, for salvation is from the Jews" (John 4:22). Nevertheless, in his parable, the goodness of a Samaritan wayfarer outshines the fear and religious meticulousness of the Levite and priest, who pass by a wounded robbery victim on the other side of the road. This Samaritan is set forth for all time as an example of caring mercy in Jesus' words: "Go and do likewise" (Luke 10:29-37).

In Acts 10 there is an account of a vision experienced by Peter which, together with an encounter immediately following it, is significant for our discussion. In a trance Peter saw a sheet let down from heaven filled with clean and unclean animals and accompanied by a voice saying, "Rise, Peter; kill and eat." When he protested that nothing common or unclean had ever entered his mouth, the voice answered, "What God has cleansed, you must not call common." This happened three times. At that very moment three men arrived at the house in Joppa where Peter was staying. They had been sent by a Roman centurion in Caesarea named Cornelius, requesting Peter to visit him. Cornelius was a devout man who feared God with all his household and generously helped the community in which he was stationed. He, too, had had a vision, telling him that his prayers and alms had ascended before God and instructing him to send for Peter in Joppa. His messengers arrived just as Peter was pondering the meaning of the vision. When he saw the gathered household and heard from Cornelius how God's angel had spoken to him, Peter began his response with, "Truly I perceive that God shows no partiality, but in every nation any one who fears him and does what is right is acceptable to him" (Acts 10:34-35).

What is the meaning of these enigmatic words? How are we to understand that anyone in every nation who "fears God" and does "what is right" is "acceptable" to God? On first glance they can be read to mean that proselytes (like Cornelius) can be accepted into the church. But the context hardly permits this understanding. The acceptance of proselytes into the church could scarcely be seen as a fulfillment of Peter's vision. The vision clearly referred to the undoing of the division between Jew and Gentile. To enlarge the area of salvation to include *also* proselytes meant in effect that it had not yet been extended beyond the Jewish orbit. Room had to be made for Gentiles *as Gentiles* in the family of God.

It is clear that Peter was committed to the broader of these two possibilities. At the same time he realized that his action would create dissension in the church in Jerusalem. When he returned to Jerusalem, "the circumcision party criticized him, saying, 'Why did you go to uncircumcised men and eat with them?' " But with the support of six witnesses whom Peter had taken along with him from Joppa to Caesarea, he convinced his critics. "When they heard this they were silenced. And they glorified God, saying, 'Then to the Gentiles also God has granted repentance unto life' " (Acts 11:1-18).

But does the inclusion of the Gentiles in the address and efficacy of the gospel do full justice to Peter's words in Acts 10:34: "Truly I perceive that God shows no partiality, but in every nation any one who fears him and does what is right is acceptable to him"? As they stand, these words make acceptability to God possible without explicit reference to the gospel. For Peter, the meaning of his words may well have been limited to the extension of the address and efficacy of the gospel to Gentiles. It had required a heavenly vision thrice repeated plus the highly unusual meeting in Caesarea and the descent of the Holy Spirit on Cornelius's company to bring him to that point.

But could it be that in the ongoing course of redemption history, Peter's vision and the opening words of his sermon point to the reality of a salvation that is effective in human areas that have not in the past been, are not now being, and may not in the future be reached by the gospel? Prophecy and vision often greatly surpass the understanding of their immediate recipients. There are in history the unreached millions, and in Scripture there are passages too often overlooked that forbid us to ignore this question. The fact of the "unreached millions" speaks for itself; the data in Scripture need to be more closely examined.

A remarkable passage in Paul's letter to the Romans, strikingly similar to Peter's words in Acts 10:34, invites attention in this connection.

> For he will render to every man according to his works: to those who by patience in well-doing seek for glory and honor and immortality, he will give eternal life; but for those who are factious and do not obey the truth, but obey wickedness, there will

> be wrath and fury . . . but glory and honor and peace for every one who does good, the Jew first and also the Greek. For God shows no partiality. (Rom. 2:6-11)

Note that both here and in Peter's declaration there is no specific reference to the relationship of the Greeks or Gentiles to the gospel. Paul would seem to be speaking here of Gentiles in their specifically Gentile relationship to God. This is supported by the fact that he is not here referring to Christian Jews, but to Jews in general, in their Old Testament capacity as people of God living under the Mosaic law. The Old Testament is a book of redemption; and it was certainly possible for members of Israel's covenant community to "seek for glory and honor and immortality" and receive the reward of eternal life. But is the same true for the Gentiles in their relationship to God? When one consults the commentaries on the Gentiles' search for "glory and honor and immortality" and the gift of eternal life bestowed upon them, the general evasiveness in dealing with the question of Gentile salvation becomes painfully evident.

Anders Nygren devotes eighteen pages of his commentary on Romans to 2:1-16. He quotes the words "To those who by patience in well-doing seek . . . he will give eternal life . . . to the Jew first and also to the Greek." But he does nothing with the meaning of this reference for the Gentiles, with the exception of the ambiguous remark, "To be sure, he will not be judged by the law; yet he will receive the proper reward for his deeds."[2] The question is, Will he receive salvation? For Nygren, the Gentiles serve the purpose of showing the severity of the judgment to which the Jews stand exposed because they have the law, whereas the Gentiles have only the "work of the law" written on their hearts. The ultimate significance of this he does not explain.

Similarly, Handley C. G. Moule, a champion of evangelical orthodoxy, devotes ten pages of his commentary on Romans to 2:1-16 without in any way coming to grips with the problem. On

2. Anders Nygren, *Commentary on Romans,* trans. Carl C. Rasmussen (Philadelphia: Muhlenberg, 1949), p. 122.

the contrary, he concludes his discussion in this manner: "Such a clause as that of ver. 14, *'when they do by nature the things of the law,'* is certainly not to be pressed, *in such a context as this,* to be an assertion that pagan morality ever actually satisfies the holy tests of the eternal Judge. Read in the whole connexion, it only asserts that the pagan acts as a moral being" [italics in original].[3] But, here again, this is not the question. The question is, Does the pagan in pursuit of glory, honor, and immortality receive eternal life or does he not?

Whatever its correctness, the *NIV Study Bible* recognizes frontally the problem that concerns us here:

> **2:6–7** Paul is not contradicting his continual emphasis in all his writings, including Romans, that a person is saved not by what he does but by faith in what Christ does for him. Rather, he is discussing the principle of judgment according to deeds. . . . If anyone persists in doing good deeds (i.e., lives a perfect life), he will receive eternal life. No one can do this, but if anyone could, God would give him life, since God judges according to what a person does.[4]

This interpretation turns Paul's entire discussion of Romans 2:1-16 into an abstract hypothetical exercise. His argument against Jewish pride is based on a hypothetical possibility that can never become a reality. For this there is certainly no exegetical basis. The "when" in 2:14 ("*When* Gentiles who have not the law do by nature what the law requires. . .") and the "if" in 2:26-27 ("*if* a man who is uncircumcised keeps the precepts of the law, will not his uncircumcision be regarded as circumcision? Then those who are physically uncircumcised but keep the law will condemn you who have the written code and circumcision but break the law") are certainly not to be regarded as abstractions that can never become realities.

A clear example of the actuality of such obedience is the cen-

3. Handley C. G. Moule, *The Epistle of St. Paul to the Romans*, 5th ed. (New York: Hodder & Stoughton, 1893), p. 66.

4. *The NIV Study Bible* (Grand Rapids: Zondervan, 1985), p. 1708.

turion who appealed to Jesus on behalf of a paralyzed servant and amazed him by his faith: "Truly, I say to you, not even in Israel have I found such faith. I tell you, many will come from east and west and sit at table with Abraham, Isaac, and Jacob in the kingdom of heaven, while the sons of the kingdom will be thrown into the outer darkness" (Matt. 8:5-13). His concern for his servant, the deference he showed to Jesus, and the trust he reposed in him—are these not things which in the eyes of heaven constituted the centurion as a seeker after glory, honor, and immortality? And is such obedience not a rebuke of Jesus' fellow Israelites in his own Galilean country whose unbelief prevented him from doing any mighty works there (Mark 6:1-6)? Could it be that we have intellectualized faith to such an extent—making it a theological affirmation and undervaluing its profoundly spiritual and human character—that we are unable to recognize it when we meet it?

The possibility of salvation outside the church and knowledge of the gospel lies in the reality of the existence of the *imago Dei.* It is out of this *imago* that the phenomenon of religion arises. Where Man, the image of God, is, there is the *sensus divinitatis,* and there is the *semen religionis.* But these are so overwhelmed by alienation from God, misconceptions about him, and the centering of our affections on ourselves, that there is no way for Man to find God by searching or by contemplation or by introspection or by losing himself in works of human merit. But although he has by his sin sealed himself off from God, he is not able as *imago Dei* to seal God out of his life. He cannot find God, but God can find him. The gospel is not the story of Man's search for God, but the story of God's seeking and claiming and finding Man. That is the Good News.

Moreover, we err when we assume that our affirmative response to God is essential to his seeking and claiming us. God's searching and claiming love may pursue us for long without our yielding ourselves to him. Many have shunned him for years before at last surrendering to his importunities. This Francis Thompson has immortalized in "The Hound of Heaven":

I fled Him, down the nights and down the days;
I fled Him, down the arches of the years;
I fled Him, down the labyrinthine ways
Of my own mind; and in the mist of tears
I hid from Him, and under running laughter.

. . . .

But with unhurrying chase,
And unperturbéd pace,
Deliberate speed, majestic instancy,
They beat—and a Voice beat
More instant than the Feet—
"All things betray thee, who betrayest Me."

Those who confess the name of Christ know the Hound of Heaven as a Father—stern yet kind, kind yet stern, and altogether patient. We know him through the gospel—the gospel speaking in the church, in the home, in the Sunday school, through friends and community, through television and radio and religious literature, and through experiences of life read in terms of what we have learned through these avenues of growth and instruction. But these voices through which God speaks to us are not heard by the "unreached millions," who thus do not have the taught knowledge of how to read the experiences of life. Nevertheless, the Hound of Heaven pursues them too:

The heavens are telling the glory of God;
and the firmament proclaims his handiwork.
Day to day pours forth speech,
and night to night declares knowledge.
There is no speech, nor are there words;
their voice is not heard;
yet their voice goes out through all the earth,
and their words to the end of the world. (Ps. 19:1-4)

And there is the voice of God in the history of tribes and peoples and nations, in their economic and political vicissitudes, and in the more personal contexts of the mother nursing her child, the father tilling the soil, the worker in the factory, the policeman on his beat, the athlete, the student, the musician, the bus driver, the philosopher, the business executive, the teacher, and the child on the playground. All these are the *imago Dei,* and they are that because they have within them the *sensus divinitatis* and the *semen religionis.*

Dare we say that God is not seeing and hearing and speaking here? That in all the concern and planning, in successes and failures, in all the honest solicitude for business and neighborhood and government and education and health care, he may not also discern—alongside of and in the noise and the bustle and the frustration, the frayed tempers and the joys of achievement—a seeking for glory and honor and immortality? And is it not his right to bestow rewards of grace as and where and how and on whom he wills? In short, did Christ die only for those who come to know him and believe in him? Did he not die for the sins of the whole world?

Is it indeed the case that the nations and peoples of the human race are held hostage for their inheriting of life eternal to the willingness or unwillingness, the ability or inability of the church to perform its missionary task? Were the ancestors of my African friend altogether dependent for their salvation on the indifference of the North African church (precisely at the time that trans-Saharan commerce was enriching its members)? Here indeed we may ask, Shall not the Judge of all the earth do right?

And can there be any doubt that along with the rewards of eternal life so given, there is also divine wrath over the hypocrisy and double-dealing and betrayal that deface the human scene? Christian guardians of morals seldom question or disapprove this. Here they see God functioning as is proper for the Judge of all the earth to do. But that he should bestow eternal life on those in the mass of humanity whom he judges to be seekers of glory, honor, and immortality—that seems too heretical to believe. Is it true that only professing Christians receive eternal life because only Christians can seek glory and honor and immortality?

The hostility in Christian circles to the idea of salvation outside of the hearing of the gospel is in some degree understandable. Particularly is this so with respect to the missionary task of the church. If those who do not know the gospel can be and are in fact being saved without such knowledge, what is the urgency for missions abroad and witness at home? Does not belief in salvation apart from the hearing of the gospel "cut the nerve" of missions? In concluding this chapter we must consider this question.

The distinguished English missionary thinker Roland Allen saw clearly both the problem here and the biblical data out of which it arises. The following series of quotations is taken from his essay "The Spirit Revealing the Need of Men":

> The apostles were profoundly conscious of the need of men for Christ, yet there are sayings in Acts, as in the gospels, which seem to make that need appear less. . . . So in the Acts, St Peter declares to Cornelius that "in every nation he that feareth God and worketh righteousness is accepted with him" (10.35). And St Paul . . . says also that God "will render to every man according to his works: to them who by patient continuance in well-doing seek for glory and honour and immortality, eternal life.". . .
>
> Now there is certainly a difficulty in reconciling . . . the apostolic assertion that men . . . can be saved only in Christ, with this more comfortable doctrine that everybody, everywhere, whatever their religious beliefs, whatever their ignorance of Christ, will yet be accepted with God, if they obey the law written in their hearts.
>
> . . . We can hardly expect people to be as fervent in the propagation of the gospel if the heathen know enough to be saved, and if it will be well with them if only they do what they now know to be right. . . . We feel almost compelled to accept one alternative or the other. . . .
>
> In the face of this difficulty it is well to return to the Acts and to read again the history recorded by St Luke. The apostolic missionaries, in his story, saw both sides of this question, they stated both sides, yet their zeal was not diminished at all. . . .
>
> The solution to the difficulty does not lie in the intellectual, but in the spiritual sphere. . . .
>
> . . . When once the Holy Spirit reveals Christ to the soul, whatever the previous religion or morality of the man may have been, he is conscious that he could not do without Christ. Rob him of

Christ, and he is robbed of all. It is wholly inconceivable that he should look back with satisfaction upon himself as he was without Christ. . . .

Yet, knowing the hopelessness of his own case without Christ, knowing the hopelessness of their case without Christ, there is, nevertheless, a hope. The Spirit of Christ is a Spirit quick to recognize and welcome signs of goodness. . . . "A cup of cold water" appears to the Spirit of love a sign of kinship with Christ; alms and prayers appear to that Spirit proofs of capacity to receive Christ. . . . Here is a soul not remote from Christ. The Spirit of Christ goes out to him, with love, and approval, and thankfulness. It welcomes him. God accepts him. "In every nation he that feareth God and worketh righteousness is accepted with him.". . .

. . . If . . . we welcome the sense of freedom from [missionary] responsibility which a benevolent optimism might seem to induce, there is little doubt that we shall explain away the sterner teaching of the apostles, and welcome their expressions of universal hope as the larger truth. . . .

Nay, more, if we allow the consideration of heathen morality and heathen religion to absolve us from the duty of preaching the gospel we are really deposing Christ from His throne in our own souls. . . . If they can do very well without Christ, then so could we. . . .

When we so speak and think we are treating the question of the salvation of men exactly as we should have treated it had Christ never appeared in the world at all. It is an essentially pre-Christian attitude, and implies that the Son of God has not been delivered for our salvation. . . .

. . . The apostles, inspired by the Holy Ghost, were troubled with no doubts whether the monotheism of the Jews or the philosophy of the Greeks were sufficient for their salvation. Filled with the Spirit, they were certain that both Jews and Greeks needed Christ, and that neither Jewish monotheism nor Greek philosophy would do instead.[5]

5. Roland Allen, *The Compulsion of the Spirit: A Roland Allen Reader*, ed. David Paton and Charles H. Long (Grand Rapids: Eerdmans, 1983), pp. 65-70 passim.

The position of Allen is clearly different from both the silence of Nygren and the dogmatic exegesis implicit in the comments of Moule and the *NIV Study Bible*. He comes squarely to grips with the declarations of Peter in Acts 10 and of Paul in Romans 2. As in all his missionary writings, Allen was dominated by the centrality of the work of the Holy Spirit in the missionary task of the church. Perhaps this explains why he did not further enlarge his exposition theologically. We shall close this chapter with some reflections in that direction.

It must be observed that the basis underlying the comments of Moule and the NIV exposition is seriously flawed. Both imply that salvation which is said to be granted to those standing outside the hearing of the gospel is necessarily a salvation granted outside the work of Christ. But since there is no name given under heaven by which Man must be saved except the name of Christ alone, such claims for salvation must be disallowed. We have emphasized in earlier chapters that no one can come to a saving knowledge of God except through the revelation of God's redemptive outreach in Christ.

But this does not mean that God in his sovereign grace cannot apply that redemption, as it were anonymously, as and when and to whom he pleases. Old Testament saints, except through little-understood intimations, had no knowledge of Christ and his work, yet they did not inherit salvation apart from him. Moreover, Israel functioned representatively as a steward of the grace of God until in Christ it could again be disseminated universally. If we so read God's continuing concern with the Gentiles during the period of the Old Testament preparation for his coming, then it is entirely permissible to see salvation for Gentiles outside the hearing of the gospel as a salvation granted in the only name given under heaven by which we must be saved.

In some Reformed circles it is a moot question whether the salvation of children dying before they reach the age of responsibility is granted only to children of believers or to all children so dying. What is clear is that *all* children are conceived and born in sin and therefore need the rebirth of a new heart, which only the Spirit of Christ can effect. Yet they are saved altogether apart from any responsible hearing of the gospel.

Special note must be taken of the objection often raised that if there is salvation outside the hearing of the gospel, the call to missions will be seriously impaired. Careful reflection about the astounding difference between salvation arising out of faith in Christ and that granted to those whose knowledge of God is limited to general revelation will invalidate such concern and in fact strengthen the calling of the church to missionary witness at home and abroad. It will introduce a dimension into the thinking of the Christian church and community and their members that can only serve to deepen appreciation for the gift of the gospel and add urgency to the sharing of it with others. Consider the following:

Those who attain to salvation apart from the knowledge and experience of the grace that is in Christ Jesus can never have a true knowledge of themselves, of the world, of the salvation that they already possess and will enjoy in its fullness in the age to come, nor of the God and Father of our Lord Jesus Christ and of all that pertains to his person and work. They are addressed only by God's general revelation. They have no God-given standard in the gift of the sacred Scripture of the Old and New Testaments for assessing either themselves or their world and its humanity or the divine power of which they can never be more than uncertainly aware.

While Paul's statement is true that what may be known of God is plain to the Gentiles and that his eternal power and deity have been clearly perceived in the things that have been made (Rom. 1:19-20), this must be read in the light of Romans 8:18-25, which declares that the forces and phenomena through which God's speaking in his general revelation takes place are themselves confused and distorted. The beauties of creation are subject to the bondage of travail and decay. Those who do not know Christ cannot know that the creation, which has been subjected to futility, waits with eager longing for the revealing of the sons of God. If even believers who have the first fruits of the Spirit groan inwardly as they await their adoption as sons through the redemption of their bodies (8:23), how much more are those in the dark and without hope who do not so much as know that a reconstitution of all things is to take place?

Moreover, the person who does not know the gospel stands outside the fellowship, the instruction, the admonition, and the comfort of the church. He does not know God the Father as Creator, nor the Son as Redeemer, nor the Holy Spirit as the Bestower of the new life which Christ purchased through his incarnation, ministry, death, resurrection, and ascent to glory and the promise of his return. He therefore does not know the basic meaning of nature, sin, and grace; and as a result he cannot know the rationale of his own existence or of the world and universe of which he is a part. Allen's words are profoundly true:

> When once the Holy Spirit reveals Christ to the soul, whatever the previous religion or morality of the man may have been, he is conscious that he could not do without Christ. Rob him of Christ, and he is robbed of all. It is wholly inconceivable that he should look back with satisfaction upon himself as he was without Christ.[6]

Finally, but not least, the knowledge that there is indeed a salvation for those who have never heard or may never hear the gospel is a great comfort for the church.

When considering the missionary outreach of the church of Christ, we may not fail to note what it did *not* achieve, as well as what it did achieve. During the first eighteen centuries the voice of the gospel was largely limited to the western peninsula of the vast Eurasian land mass. A glance at a world map will show how very small this evangelized area is. During the first seven centuries the North African church was strong, but from then on it succumbed increasingly to the weight of Muslim religion and its Arab culture.

From the sixteenth century on, Roman Catholic missions were active in Central and South America and in the Orient, but the close linkage between church and crown greatly blunted their impact. North America, Asia as a whole, Africa south of the

6. Allen, pp. 67-68.

Sahara, much of South America, and all the native people of Australia and Oceania had to wait until a later time to hear the gospel.

When the gospel proclamation finally became worldwide in the nineteenth and twentieth centuries, its outreach never touched all its target, and it has never kept up with the universal population increase. Moreover, in the present century, as earlier noted, large Christian areas have been lost to secularism and Communism with their atheistic ideologies. This in broad strokes describes the gospel penetration from Pentecost to the present time.

During the time of missionary outreach, work that was undertaken was often limited to a small fraction of the church. In many areas the sense of missionary urgency did not take hold. In those areas where it did, the missionaries not only had to cope with the difficulties of mastering languages wholly new to them, but often failed adequately to relate the message of the gospel to the cultures of the peoples that they approached. In many cases transmission of the cultural outlook of the sending church or missionary society was seen as missionary wisdom. It was not until well into the twentieth century that the more relevant witness of the newly founded churches began to impact massively on their own peoples.

Moreover, there was during the millennia preceding Pentecost that vast humanity outside of Israel to which no knowledge of salvation was made known.

Is it therefore not a great comfort for the church to know that, during the centuries that awaited the coming of Christ and during the years when the gospel was only gradually and partially reaching the peoples and nations of the world, God's arm was not shortened so that it could not save?

We cannot contemplate how the church of Christ has carried out the Great Commission without a profound sense of its inadequacy. But God's saving intent is not held hostage either by the deterioration of his image in mankind or by the never more than partial faithfulness of the church in making his gospel known. Here we must try to understand both the graciousness of God and the sense of unworthiness of his people as these are revealed in Revelation 4.

John's vision shows him God seated on his throne in heaven in a setting of inexpressible majesty and power. Around him are seated twenty-four elders with golden crowns on their heads. They represent the congregation of the twelve tribes of Israel and the church of Christ founded on the witness of the twelve apostles. As they join with other voices and powers in giving glory and honor and thanks to him who is seated on the throne, who lives forever and ever, the twenty-four elders are overcome with a sense of their unworthiness. Falling down before the throne, they cast their crowns at his feet thus to testify that the honor they have been accorded belongs not to them but to him alone.

Thus will the people of God in the eternal mansions that await them rejoice in the saving power of God, who wrought a salvation that reached immeasurably beyond their own furthest vision and beyond their utmost exertion.

Chapter VIII

The Ad Hoc God

Now therefore let me alone, that . . . I may consume them; but of you I will make a great nation.

Exodus 32:10

A characteristic feature of the human situation is the need to respond to wholly unforeseen happenings. No aspect of life is exempt from the unexpected and the abnormal, be it good or ill. Equally characteristic is the demonstrated resourcefulness of the race in reacting to changes that are thrust upon it. The adequacy of the response may be minimal, but it is seldom wholly wanting, and often it is very great and productive. Adaptability to change is obviously rooted deeply in the human being in its individual and collective forms. Versatility and ingenuity mark the entity that is Man.

Adaptability to change would have been a human characteristic even if sin had not entered in to disrupt life. It would appear to be a quality native to Man for the successful discharge of the divine mandate to have dominion over the earth and to subdue it. Since this mandate of dominion is inseparably associated with Man's creation in the image of God, we can hardly fail to ask whether this adaptability is also characteristic of the life of God in relation to the created universe. Specifically, is Man's competence for adaptation and adjustment also a reflection of the *imago Dei?* Or is this feature in Man simply a higher manifestation of a similar if reduced trait in the animal world?

The problem here is not a predominantly anthropological one. We are not in the present discussion concerned so much with the doctrine of the image of God in its significance for Man as with the significance of the *imago Dei* concept for our understanding of God. Jesus said, "He who has seen me has seen the Father" (John 14:9). The Psalmist wrote, "He who planted the ear, does he not hear? He who formed the eye, does he not see?" (94:9). In such passages the creaturely is descriptive of the Creator. May we not similarly ask whether he who created Man to be so wonderfully adaptable and positively responsive to change is himself possessed of such adaptability and resilience?

In the development of mainline Protestant and Roman Catholic doctrine there appears to be no room for surprise or adaptation in the life of the Creator and Redeemer God. The whole of created reality is seen as standing before his all-seeing eye and all-knowing mind in an ever-present eternal simultaneity, in which no before or after can exist. Since a humanity for which past and future do not exist is inconceivable and since it is of the highest importance that our understanding of God in respect of his relationship to temporal sequence be scripturally valid, it is necessary to consider and assess this theological tradition.

The long regnant Christian theological position with respect to God's temporal relationship to the world was set by St. Augustine (A.D. 354–430), bishop of Hippo in the Roman province of North Africa. His profound and devout mind left so indelible a mark on the history of the church in the West and on the civilization that it influenced that both the Roman Catholic and the Protestant wings of the church claim him as their own.

Augustine taught that God, dwelling in eternity, is not bound by time. He knows no past (in the sense of that which is no more) and faces no future (in the sense of that which is not yet). Rather, God lives the fullness of his life in an eternal present, a never-becoming, never-changing, never-ceasing *now,* which always and exclusively *is.*

> What man, then, is there who can comprehend that wisdom by which God knows all things in such wise that neither what we call things past are past therein, nor what we call things future are therein waited for as coming, as though they were absent, but both past and future with things present are all present: nor yet are things thought severally, so that thought passes from one to another, but all things simultaneously are at hand in one glance.[1]

Augustine acknowledged that he derived this understanding of God's eternity from the Greek philosopher Plato (428–347 B.C.), who in turn had taken it over from an earlier Greek thinker, Parmenides. Plato wrote,

> When the Father who begat the world saw the image which he had made of the eternal gods moving and living, he rejoiced. . . . Wherefore he made an image of eternity which is time, having uniform motion according to number, parted into months and days and years. . . . These all apply to becoming in time, and have no meaning in relation to eternal nature, which ever is and never was or will be; for the unchangeable is never older or younger, and when we say that he "was" or "will be," we are mistaken, for these words are applicable only to becoming, and not to true being.[2]

We shall return to the significance of this conjunction of Greek philosophy and Christian theology. Here we wish to emphasize that Augustine determined the conception of God's eternity on the basis of a purely pagan intellectual apprehension, in which the Creator-Redeemer God revealed in the Scriptures played no role whatever. So representative and authoritative a figure as John Calvin wrote,

> When we attribute foreknowledge to God, we mean that all things always were, and perpetually remain, under his eyes, so that to his

1. Augustine, *The Trinity,* XV.7.13.
2. Plato, *Timaeus,* 37C-38A.

> knowledge there is nothing future or past, but all things are present. And they are present in such a way that he not only conceives them through ideas, as we have before us those things which our minds remember, but he truly looks upon them and discerns them as things placed before him [to see]. And this foreknowledge is extended throughout the universe to every creature. (*Institutes,* III.xxi.5)

William C. Kneale, writing in *The Encyclopedia of Philosophy,* describes the view of St. Thomas Aquinas that "there are two marks of eternity, namely, that the eternal has neither beginning nor end and that eternity contains no succession, being all at once *(tota simul existens)*" as "a rendering of words Parmenides had used over 17 centuries earlier."[3] Herman Bavinck wrote that God's knowledge "is one, simple and unchangeable, eternal. He knows all things at once, simultaneously, from eternity, and everything stands eternally present before his eyes."[4]

The similarity of Augustine's view of eternity to that of Plato is not accidental. His theology is the climax of three and a half centuries of reflection on the gospel by theologians whose mind-set had at least formally been influenced profoundly by the Hellenic manner of philosophical thinking. To find unity in all the bewildering diversities in life and in nature was a basic drive in the Greek mind. Its various schools of thought engaged in endless analyses, classifications, comparisons, and syntheses.

In the flowering of Greek philosophy in the systems of Plato and his equally famous disciple Aristotle (384–322 B.C.), one basic theme controlled all thought: the distinction, variously expressed, between the uncreated and the created, soul and body, spirit and matter, eternity and time, and—especially in Plato—ideas (in eternity) and their copies (in time and matter).

Fundamental in Plato's philosophy was the belief that all that is good and noble, all that is ultimately real and abiding, lies rooted in the eternal world of the ideas. By "idea" here is not

3. William C. Kneale, "Eternity," *The Encyclopedia of Philosophy*, vol. 3 (New York: Macmillan, 1967), p. 65.

4. Bavinck, *Gereformeerde Dogmatiek,* 2:188.

meant a conception or a thought, but a spiritual reality or entity which has its own independent existence, indestructible being, and character. All that is temporal are copies of eternal ideas. Evil inheres in matter and in temporal circumscription. Consequently, every copy of an idea, material or nonmaterial, inevitably constitutes a fusion of the perfect with the imperfect. Nonbeing is essentially bound up in the best of copies. The body is a "prison-house of the soul." Therefore death is a liberation in which the soul returns to its proper realm of the ideas.

The wise men of Greece listened to Paul on the Areopagus until he spoke of a man whom God had appointed to judge the world, of which God had given assurance to all "by raising him from the dead" (Acts 17:31). At that point the party broke up. Some mocked; some said they would see Paul another time. To be resurrected from the dead was to return to the body, and what greater mishap could befall one than that?

Strictly speaking, according to that tradition, the world of being is the eternal world of ideas, of which the Idea of the Good is the apex. In that world there is no past, no future; there is no "has been," no "will be," no "becoming," for that existence is a constant, eternally present *being*. The world of humanity and nature is the world of time with all its flux and change, the world in which only death has a word of hope and liberation.

During the first four centuries after Christ, Greek categories of thought remained influential in philosophical discourse in the Mediterranean basin. It was natural for Christian theologians to avail themselves of concepts and terms current among thinkers of the day. William C. Kneale writes that

> by the end of the fifth century A.D. there was nothing at all strange in the use of Platonic thought for the exposition of Christianity. Thus St. Augustine, when commenting in his *De Civitate Dei* on the sentence in Genesis "God saw that it was good," refers explicitly to the passage of [Plato's] *Timaeus*. . . .[5]

5. William C. Kneale, "Time and Eternity in Theology," *Proceedings of the Aristotelian Society* (1961).

Earlier, Adolf von Harnack wrote that "in the Alexandrian school of catechists [ca. 200] the whole of Greek science was taught and made to serve the purpose of Christian apologetics."[6]

As Christianity gained in favor and power in the Roman empire during the second and third centuries and became its official religion under Constantine in the fourth, the way was open for Christian apologists to set forth the faith polemically and didactically. They expounded the gospel in terms of concepts molded in the forums of philosophical debate. Words like *love, salvation, savior, revelation, sin, forgiveness, church, justification, lord* received a Christian content they had never had before. At the same time—and this is the point we wish to emphasize—words and concepts readily taken over from the Greek and "baptized" by the Christian community did not always lose the weight of meaning they bore in the Greek milieu. Thus subtly—and sometimes not so subtly—non-Christian philosophical ideas entered into Christian perception.

That is precisely what happened in the Christian adoption of the Greek contrast of eternity and time. In the scale of values, eternity is superior; time is inferior. Eternity is being; time is becoming. The one abides; the other passes away. The one is a heavenly, divine dimension; the other, an earthly, humanly perceived continuum.

But this is Christianly unacceptable. In the biblical view of things, time is of the essence. To say creation, to say salvation, to say incarnation, to say kingdom of God, to say Christ, to say consummation is to say time. To say time is to say history; and to say history is to say *eschatos* and eschatology, the End and the doctrine of the End. Whether in the state of innocence or in the state of sin, duration—the succession of moments in the experience of past and present and the anticipation of moments in the future—is the God-given milieu in which Man lives his life and

6. Adolf von Harnack, *History of Dogma,* 7 vols., trans. Neil Buchanan (New York: Dover, 1961), 2:323.

the whole world with him. Indeed, to say time is to say God in his everlasting duration.

Introducing its discussion of *aion* and *aionion* ("eternity" and "eternal"), Kittel's *Theological Dictionary of the New Testament* notes that Plato's conception was continued in the early first-century Jewish philosopher Philo. He in turn greatly influenced the religious and philosophical speculation of the Gnostics, in the midst of whose teachings the earliest church lived. For *TDNT,* however, there is no doubt that the biblical view differs radically from the Greek understanding of eternity. The Old Testament teaches that

> the unending eternity of God and the time of the world, which is limited by its creation and conclusion, are contrasted with one another. Eternity is thought of as unending time . . . and the eternal being of God is represented as pre-existence and post-existence. . . .
>
> The NT took over the OT and Jewish view of divine eternity. . . . Statements concerning the eternal being and action of God are thus expressed in terms of pre- and post-. . . . To this context there also belongs the doctrine of the pre-existence of Christ.[7]

In 1945, thirteen years after this article first appeared in German, Oscar Cullmann published his important work *Christ and Time.* He writes, "If we wish to grasp the Primitive Christian idea of eternity, we must strive above all to think in as unphilosophical a manner as possible."[8] That is, we must obtain our ideas of time and eternity from the Bible. There we find "time in its entire unending extension, which is unlimited in both the backward and the forward direction." This is the fullest use of the word eternity as it is used in the Bible and as such "comes into consideration only as an attribute of God." But there is also "the time that extends beyond the end of the present age," which "in the

7. Gerhard Kittel, ed. *Theological Dictionary of the New Testament*, trans. G.W. Bromiley (Grand Rapids: Eerdmans, 1964), 1:201-2.

8. Oscar Cullmann, *Christ and Time,* trans. Floyd V. Filson (London: SCM Press, 1951), p. 64.

forward direction . . . is unlimited, unending, and only in this sense . . . eternal." Human time therefore may be said to correspond with God's time in that it has no end, while God's time is both without beginning and without end.[9]

In an essay on "God Everlasting" Nicholas Wolterstorff writes that "the patterns of classical Greek thought are incompatible with the pattern of biblical thought. And in facing the issue of God everlasting versus God eternal [in the Platonic sense] we are dealing with the fundamental pattern of biblical thought."[10]

The biblical and Greek conceptions of time and eternity are wholly incommensurable. They have no common basis: each in its very nature excludes the other.

It could be argued that the Greek idea of eternity is reflected in our ability to draw the past, the present, and to a certain extent the future into a unitary present in the combined mental activities of memory, awareness, and anticipation. But even such an effort requires duration to think it. Moreover, anticipation is never quite the same as the reality that will be experienced. Heraclitus, another early Greek philosopher, expressed it classically in his famous river figure: All things flow, and we never step into the same river twice.

The difference between the Greek philosophical conception and the Jewish religious idea, particularly as reflected in the Old and the New Testaments, is important to note in the context of this chapter. Philosophy is basically a reaching out of the human mind for the intellectual understanding of reality. Religion is basically a reaching out of the soul for the spiritual apprehension of God as he has revealed himself. The essence of the Greek effort was intellectual and therefore abstract and impersonal. Its concern was with concept, levels of being, and their relation to each other. The Jewish concern was with Man's relationship to

9. Cullmann, p. 48.

10. Nicholas Wolterstorff, "God Everlasting," in *God and the Good: Essays in Honor of Henry Stob*, ed. Clifton Orlebeke and Lewis Smedes (Grand Rapids: Eerdmans, 1975), p. 183.

God in terms of revelation, prayer, sacrifice, praise, and, above all, with becoming reconciled to offended deity.

Even so, the Jewish religious genius for apprehending the divine is not in itself superior in value to the Greek intellectual genius for comprehending reality. Man cannot by seeking find out God, whether the search is conducted by the mind or by the soul.

The uniqueness of Israel lies rather in God's choice of it as the vehicle of his redemptive revelation to humanity. Their Semitic origins probably disposed the Jews to religious rather than to philosophical inquiry into the nature of ultimate reality. Nevertheless, their concern to commune not with the God of the philosophers, but with the God of Abraham, Isaac, and Jacob, was less a unilateral subjective exertion than a spontaneous response of the soul to divine revelation. And this response was one of person to Person, and as such from the whole Man to the whole divinity. Through the prophets, God spoke to Israel from the fullness of his being to the fullness of his image in them, and they in like manner were called so to respond.

Religion, therefore, is *imago Dei* seeking fellowship with its divine Original in response to the self-disclosure of the Original. A basic element in this self-disclosure is that through the act of creation God not only introduced Man into personal fellowship with himself but also in so doing introduced him into the temporal flow of God's own existence. God's time and our time are therefore not antithetical but rather homogeneous, though with the ineradicable difference that for Man time began with his creation, whereas for God it always was. From a purely qualitative point of view, therefore, God's time, like our time, has duration. Temporally as well as otherwise, mankind is *imago Dei.*

Redemptive revelation corresponds in a crucial respect to God's revelation in creation. As God addressed unfallen Man in the context of an unfallen creation, so he addresses his fallen *imago Dei* in the context of the fallen *vestigia Dei.* Therefore the whole cosmos continues to be invested with religious significance. All of nature has something to say in terms of "God talk."

"The heavens are telling the glory of God; and the firmament proclaims his handiwork" (Ps. 19:1). "The voice of the Lord is upon the waters; the God of glory thunders" (Ps. 29:3). "Consider the lilies. . . . If God so clothes the grass of the field . . . will he not much more clothe you, O men of little faith?" (Matt. 6:28, 30). The entirety of Man's being and his whole earthly and cosmic habitat remain means by which God addresses Man and Man responds to God. All that is familiar to us as *anthropoi* (the Greek word for human beings) remains creationally and becomes redemptively an avenue of revelation. That is what the theologians mean when they say that God's revelation to Man is *anthropomorphic* (that is, "taking human form").

God's anthropomorphic condescension to our human limitations finds its highest and most sublime expression in the incarnation of the Son of God in the birth of Jesus in Bethlehem. "In the beginning was the Word, and the Word was with God, and the Word was God. He was in the beginning with God . . . and the Word became flesh and dwelt among us" (John 1:1-2, 14). Here we are no longer dealing with a figurative—however meaningful and relevant—anthropomorphism, but with one of such an existential sort that in Christ the Word became a human being "and dwelt among us."

He dwelt among us so truly that he lived our life, knew our joys, suffered our pains, experienced our sorrows, and died our death. And this he did as the unique *imago Dei,* uniting us as Mediator to the God from whom all things come and to whom all things return. The conception of God's anthropomorphic coming to us, first in our creation and then in our redemption, is not just a convenient device for divine-human interaction but arises from the very heart and being of God himself.

We are now in position to return to the question with which this chapter began: does the human ability to adapt to change reflect something similar in the being of the divine Original? Can God be confronted by the unexpected? Can he adapt himself to an unforeseen situation? More fundamentally, is God's future time-flow confronted with possible obstacles which may threaten the ends he envisioned in creating and subsequently redeeming the world? There is in the Bible no theological, much less a philosophical, discussion of such questions. There are, however, meaningful indications pointing to an answer.

Whether we understand the account of creation in Genesis as a literal record of the events by which God brought the universe and mankind into being or as a figurative or symbolic depiction of his creative action, all Christians agree that God's own evaluation of his work is to be understood quite literally: "And God saw everything that he had made, and behold, it was very good" (Gen. 1:31). What God saw as the final result of his creative action was the complete and flawless embodiment of the divine intention. The stage was set for unimpeded deployment of the limitless material and spiritual potential he had implanted in the vast cosmic framework. And at the head of all stood his vicegerent mankind, male and female, completely equipped to understand and master all that was given it to superintend.

What we call "the flawless embodiment of the divine intention" may seem to be contradicted by the fall of the "good" creation early on, from the fullness of life to the abyss of death. This possibility existed from the beginning, however, precisely because Adam and Eve as representative of mankind were free with the freedom that characterizes God himself. To be truly *imago Dei* Man has to be free. For obedience to be truly obedience, for love to be truly love, it must be willed, spontaneous, gladly given. The modest "it was very good" echoes the restrained craftsman's pride in work well done. But it was spoken in the consciousness of the possibility of failure at the heart of the undertaking. Hence the ominous word of warning: "Of the tree of the knowledge of good and evil you shall not eat, for in the day that you eat of it you shall die" (Gen. 2:17).

As it stands, this statement is difficult to understand, for in the good creation there had been no human death or alienation from God, which is the ultimate meaning of death. It may in any case be fairly assumed that the significance of these words was understood and that therefore the reference to moral darkness was not an innocent mistake.

Even so, there is no ground whatever for believing that Man's disobedience was the effectuation or fulfillment or fruition of a divine foreordination. God's plan was obviously one that envisaged obedience. Moreover, creation in the image of God who is holy, the happy environment that constituted the human habitat, the challenging task of subjecting the whole earth to the will of Man-under-God, together with the frank warning recorded in Genesis 2:17, tilted the odds in the direction of continued fellowship between God and Man. Therefore, even if we cannot in the strictest sense of the word speak of the fall as "surprising" God, it is certainly wholly legitimate on the basis of the biblical givens to say that God was profoundly disappointed. The divine chagrin expressed itself in four judicial acts. The serpent, the woman, and the yielding man all received punishment appropriate to their respective characters, and the human pair was driven out of the garden of God.

No further sin is reported of the parents of the race, but their offspring did not follow in the footsteps of their restraint. Among these the Cainites were chief, but soon the Sethites embraced their example, until God saw that "the wickedness of man was great in the earth, and that every imagination of the thoughts of his heart was only evil continually" (Gen. 6:5). At this point God's containment of his displeasure broke out into emotional vehemence:

> The Lord was sorry that he had made man on the earth, and it grieved him to his heart. So the Lord said, "I will blot out man whom I have created from the face of the ground, man and beast and creeping things and birds of the air, for I am sorry that I have made them." (Gen. 6:6-7)

It appears that after Man's fall into sin the highly ordered plan of creation was followed by an ad hoc improvisation to salvage the remnants that survived the catastrophe. Consider the contrast between God's actions before the fall and after it. On the chaos of a dark and watery expanse, the Spirit of God sought to impose an ordered physical and spiritual structure. This was effected in six days of creation, clearly divided into two sections of three days each: the fourth day complemented the first, the fifth the second, and the sixth the third. Light was called day; darkness was called night; waters were separated from waters, with a firmament between them. The waters under the firmament were called seas, and the land was called earth. Lights in the heavens separated day from night and became signs for seasons, for days, and for years. All plant and animal life reproduced itself, "each according to its kind." When this had all been achieved, with Man the *imago Dei,* the capstone of the vast structure, to govern and administer the whole, the Creator expressed his "very good."

From this point on there is no longer discernible the picture of an ordered, unhindered Creator in whose hand all things are pliant matter and willing spirit in the execution of a plan-in-process-of-actualization. There seems rather to be a series of ad hoc actions, determined in each case by Man's conduct. The first effort to deal with the broken God-Man relationship foundered on the sin of Man, which, going from bad to worse, led to the judgment of the flood. The second, building on the one family saved from it, soon witnessed a harvest of disobedience that inevitably followed the proliferation of the same kind of humanity that had brought on the deluge.

But now disobedience was more sophisticated and concentrated. Instead of scattering over the earth to subdue it, according to the law of their created being, people organized themselves to prevent this. As a means of unifying their society they built a city and in it as its distinguishing feature "a tower with its top in the heavens." This was frustrated by God's intervention to "'confuse their language, that they may not understand one another's speech.' So the Lord scattered them abroad from there over the face of all the earth, and they left off building the city" (Gen. 11:1-9). Thus came to an end the second attempt to reconcile Man to God.

The third undertaking differed radically from the first two. In it God's redemptive concern was concentrated on one man,

Abraham, and his descendants. In setting apart Abraham and his posterity, God abandoned direct universal redemptive effort in order to prepare an effective universal redemptive outreach within a context of particularism. While not leaving them without a witness to the Creator, God "allowed all the nations to walk in their own ways" (Acts 14:16). Nevertheless, the entire history of Israel was conceived in and flowed out of a divine matrix of the profoundest universal redemptive concern:

> Now the Lord said to Abram, "Go from your country and your kindred and your father's house to the land that I will show you . . . ; and by you all the families of the earth shall bless themselves" [or, "in you all the families of the earth will be blessed"]. (Gen. 12:1-3)

This is a watershed passage not only in the Old Testament, but in the Bible as a whole. It constitutes the beginning of the Jewish people and as such the laying of the Old Testament foundation for the Christ event. It is often forgotten that Abraham was a typical member of the post-flood humanity. A "wandering Aramean" was the father of Israel (Deut. 26:5). Likewise, it is much forgotten that the Lord instructed Moses to tell the Pharaoh, "Thus says the Lord, Israel is my first-born son" (Exod. 4:22), a full and primary member, therefore, in God's great family of nations. Matthew 1:1-17 traces the genealogy of Jesus back to Abraham, thereby stressing the particularism of his history; Luke, with the Gentiles importantly in mind, traces his genealogy of Jesus through Abraham back to Adam (3:23-38), thereby emphasizing his universal significance. Jesus' favorite self-designation was not Son of Abraham or Son of David but Son of Man.

The redemptive concentration was focused so centrally on Abraham as a person, on his family and immediate offspring, tribally on his later offspring, nationally on their political and social organization, religiously on priesthood, temple, and prophecy, geographically on the Palestinian homeland, that in the course of the centuries Israel forgot altogether that its office was to be a channel of blessing to all men. It quite misunderstood the representative intent of Amos's "You only have I known of all the families of the earth" (3:2).

Yet early in its history even this third redemptive endeavor came to the verge of disaster. When Israel encamped at Sinai after its liberation fom Egypt, God called Moses to him on the mountain to give him two tables of stone engraved with the Ten Commandments. While Moses was absent from the camp, his brother Aaron yielded to the demands of the people to make an idol for them. He called for gold to be given him, and, in the words of his own incredible report to his horrified brother, "So they gave it to me, and I threw it into the fire, and there came out this calf" (Exod. 32:24). While Moses still stood before him, the Lord had seen Israel worshiping the golden calf. In overflowing indignation he said to Moses, "Now therefore let me alone, that my wrath may burn hot against them and I may consume them; but of you I will make a great nation" (Exod. 32:10). But Moses remonstrated with equal though gentler passion:

> "Turn from thy fierce wrath, and repent of this evil against thy people. Remember Abraham, Isaac, and Israel, thy servants, to whom thou didst swear by thine own self . . . 'I will multiply your descendants as the stars of heaven, and all this land that I have promised I will give to your descendants, and they shall inherit it for ever.'" And the Lord repented of the evil which he thought to do to his people. (Exod. 32:12-14)

Here is ad hoc in hardly comparable degree.

Consider, too, the Lord's excoriation of Israel because of its follies recorded, later, in the first ten chapters of Hosea, followed by these words of unsurpassed pathos:

> How can I give you up, O Ephraim!
>   How can I hand you over, O Israel!
> How can I make you like Admah!
>   How can I treat you like Zeboiim!
> My heart recoils within me,
>   my compassion grows warm and tender.
> I will not execute my fierce anger,

> I will not again destroy Ephraim,
> for I am God and not man. (11:8-9)

But most of all must we consider that greatest of all ad hoc dimensions: the divine intention to incarnate the Son of God in the form of a man. Behold him emptying himself of his prerogatives and glory, taking the form of a servant and humbling himself to death on a cross (Phil. 2:5-8). Is even the incarnation divine ad hoc? Yes, and not only that. The whole of the redemptive process from fall to new creation is an ad hoc undertaking. It does not flow out of God's work as Creator. The work of Christ was "not of this creation" (Heb. 9:11). The fall of Man into sin was a catastrophic derailment of both the nature and the purpose of creation. The ad hoc function of redemption is the restoration of creation to its original grandeur, deepened and made even more glorious by the process and experience of redemption.

The ad hoc function of redemption is signalized by St. Paul in his remarkable reference to the Mediator's completion of his task:

> Then comes the end, when he delivers the kingdom to God the Father after destroying every rule and every authority and power. . . . When all things are subjected to him, then the Son himself will also be subjected to him who put all things under him, that God may be everything to every one. (1 Cor. 15:24, 28)

The authority given to Christ to perform his mediatorial task was a temporary authority, a power given for a time. However long the time required to complete his work, it is of limited extent. "Then comes the end, when he delivers the kingdom to God the Father." At that time Christ, the King of kings and Lord of lords, will surrender his royal power and will resume the ordinary role of his divine sonship, as the King James Version puts it more poetically, "that God may be all in all." Then the Father will behold neither creation, his first work, nor redemption, his ad hoc work, but he will see *redeemed creation* that will never be despoiled again.

However, the judgment that redemption is to be seen as an ad hoc, unplanned, unexpected, remedial divine action would seem to be contradicted by the New Testament's frequent association of the word "eternal" or equivalent expressions with the work of redemption. The following are representative passages:

> . . . this Jesus, delivered up according to the definite plan and foreknowledge of God . . . (Acts 2:23)

> For those whom he foreknew he also predestined to be conformed to the image of his Son. (Rom. 8:29)

> Blessed be the God and Father of our Lord Jesus Christ . . . even as he chose us in him before the foundation of the world. (Eph. 1:3-4)

> . . . according to the eternal purpose which [God] has realized in Christ Jesus our Lord. (Eph. 3:11)

> . . . God . . . saved us and called us with a holy calling . . . in virtue of his own purpose and the grace which he gave us in Christ Jesus ages ago, and now has manifested. (2 Tim. 1:8-10)

> . . . to further the faith of God's elect and their knowledge of the truth . . . in hope of eternal life which God, who never lies, promised ages ago and at the proper time manifested in his word. (Titus 1:1-3)

> . . . [Authority was given to the beast over] every one whose name has not been written before the foundation of the world in the book of life of the Lamb that was slain. (Rev. 13:7-8)

We cannot stress God's ad hoc actions in the course of effecting his work of redemption if we do not take passages like these into serious account. On the point at issue, they are plain in indicating, in themselves and even more in the context of the New Testament as a whole, that God did indeed know "the end from the beginning" (Isa. 46:10).

But this does not undo or neutralize the substantial body of scriptural evidence that God is again and again presented as painfully surprised by unexpected events, which he then addresses and deals with in an ad hoc manner. Theology in which the Augustinian view of eternity prevails necessarily subordinates this ad hoc data, either by creating a hiatus between eternity and history or by dismissing the ad hoc material as an "anthropomorphism" with no counterpart in the life of God. The Westminster Confession shows what becomes of human freedom when history is read in the light of the then-prevailing view of eternity:

> God from all eternity did, by the most wise and holy counsel of his own will, freely and unchangeably ordain whatsoever comes to pass: yet so, as thereby is neither God the author of sin, nor is violence offered to the will of the creatures, nor is the liberty or contingency of second causes taken away, but rather established. (III.1)

But this is not a realistic facing of the problem of God's relationship to history and the humanity that constitutes its *dramatis personae.* The exoneration of God from all responsibility for the appearance of sin, although he ordained it, and the declaration of culpability for sin on the part of mankind, which did not exist when it was ordained, was for centuries seen as the height of biblical insight and theological wisdom. But the doctrine of divine sovereignty so understood has had its day. Its course has been run, and ways must be found to revitalize the Reformed vision.

We must continue our thinking and discussion about God's relationship to the world by dismissing as altogether invalid the basically pagan principle that lies at the root of the traditional Christian conception of eternity. In its place we must accept the idea of endlessly extended time—for God without beginning and without end, for Man without end but with beginning. This gives us as a starting point the element of time—common to both God and Man—to work with. Within this common temporal dimension we have a further commonality, namely, the fact of the shared similarity inhering in Man's being *imago Dei* and in God as the Prototype of the *imago.*

This commonality, however, has its limits. A disparity separates God and Man that neither can remove. God is God, and Man is Man. God's thoughts are not our thoughts; neither are his ways our ways. For as the heavens are higher than the earth, so are his ways higher than our ways, and his thoughts than our thoughts (Isa. 55:8-9). Yet this unbridgeable divine-human disparity does not prevent the most intimate kind of communication: "Come now, let us reason together, says the Lord: though your sins are like scarlet, they shall be as white as snow; though they are red like crimson, they shall become like wool" (Isa. 1:18). Indeed, so divinely manageable is the divine-human inequality that the Son of God "became flesh and dwelt among us, full of grace and truth; we have beheld his glory, glory as of the only Son of the Father" (John 1:14). Therefore the divine-human imbalance is not a divine-human antithesis. It is more a question of dimension: a rivulet is not a river, a cat is not a lion, a pine tree is not a California redwood, yet the commonality of each pair is obvious.

But the illustration must not mislead us. *Watercourse* describes both river and rivulet, *feline* both cat and lion, *tree* both redwood and pine. Each duo belongs to a common family, and each belongs to it in full measure. But God and his human image do not belong to a common family. They are separated by a quality called transcendence. Reinhold Niebuhr speaks an important word here:

> From the standpoint of an understanding of human nature, the significance of a religion of revelation lies in the fact that both the transcendence of God over, and his intimate relation to, the world are equally emphasized. . . . The transcendent God of Biblical faith makes Himself known in the finite and historical world. . . . In this divine transcendence the spirit of man finds a home in which it can understand its stature of freedom. But there it also finds the limits of its freedom, the judgment which is spoken against it and, ultimately, the mercy which makes such a judgment sufferable.[11]

Therefore, in God we live and move and have our being; we are even his offspring (Acts 17:28), while yet he dwells in un-

11. Reinhold Niebuhr, *The Nature and Destiny of Man,* Vol. 1: *Human Nature* (New York: Charles Scribner's Sons, 1964), p. 126.

approachable light (1 Tim. 6:16). Immanence and transcendence are strangely blended in God, who made the heavens and the earth, and his offspring Man as vicegerent over them. To accept the unalterable fact of our createdness, in which we pray without reserve as our Lord taught us, "Our Father who art in heaven, hallowed be your name . . ." (Matt. 6:9), and at the same time "find a home" in God's unapproachableness—this happy comfortable union of opposites is the mark of reconciled and therefore genuine humanity.

In seeking to harmonize the ad hoc actions of the God who is immanent in the world with the unchanging purposes of the God who is transcendent to it, we will be well served by making a fundamental distinction between the unchanging goals of creation and redemption set by God in his transcendence and the ad hoc actions of God in the historical process as these are effected in his immanence. Much could be written about the relationship between ultimate goal and temporal process. For the purpose of this chapter, however, I confine myself to one observation, which is basic to all else if we would speak Christianly.

The danger to which our human nature exposes us as we endeavor to understand the relationship between God's immanence and his transcendence is that we shall seek to *comprehend* it. It is certainly our duty to be aware of the conjunction between the two dimensions in our study of God's Word and in our observation and experience of them. What is at issue is the manner in which we seek to crystallize our awareness. The Western mind, deeply influenced by the classic Greek philosophical tradition on the one hand and by the secularism of our own time on the other, does not acknowledge the limits the Creator-creature relationship places on the thought of Man. It indulges this pride, which tends only to death.

If comprehension cannot be the fruit of studied awareness, to what then should the fact of the tension between God's immanence in the world and his transcendence to it lead? It should lead to such recognition and acceptance of both as is becoming to a *created being* who knows herself or himself to be a part of mankind, that is, a participant in the *image of God—created* and therefore finite, in the *image* of God and therefore touching *without* intrusion the fringes of infinity. This is to discover true knowledge and to experience the peace of God that passes all understanding.

Chapter IX

The Split of the *Imago Dei* in Reformed Theology

> *The rest of mankind God was pleased . . . to pass by, and to ordain them to dishonor and wrath for their sin, to the praise of his glorious justice.*
>
> Westminster Confession III.7

It is remarkable that Jesus, who was *par excellence* the *imago Dei,* is not in the four gospels identified with those works which the Genesis creation account most associates with Man's chief tasks as image of God. He did not contribute to the increase of the human race, he did not subdue the earth, and he did not exercise dominion over the fish of the sea, the birds of the air, or the animals and insects that live and move upon the earth. He was and sought to be no more than a rabbi in Israel.

It is not that he did not have the power to do any of these things. He turned water into wine; he healed the sick; he raised the dead; he restored the lame and the blind. He also tamed the waves of the Sea of Galilee and led a school of fish into fishermen's nets. But these activities did not, so to speak, *define* him. Rather, they lent credence and support to his rabbinical ministry. He went about teaching and preaching the kingdom of God, "doing good and healing all that were oppressed by the devil, for God was with him" (Acts 10:38).

Jesus was not a scientist, a statesman, a philosopher, an artist, a musician, a literary figure, a builder. He evinced no interest in any of these callings. Except in the area of religion he made no contributions to executing what is commonly called "the cultural mandate" laid upon Man by his creation. Even in the dimension of religion it is hardly appropriate, from a Christian point of view, to say that he "made a contribution." At this point we can say only that in the area of Man's relationship to God he laid the foundation for its restoration in integrity.

It was tempting to entitle this chapter "Jesus Was Not an Engineer." No designation of expertise, it seems to me, so fittingly describes the Maker of the physical universe as "Engineer." From the infinitely minute DNA molecular structure that determines heredity to the uniform ordinances that govern the life of the galactic universe, all physical existence is subject to unvarying and unsparing law and consists everywhere of identical elements of matter. God created this macro-micro universe through the instrumentality of the Son of God, who in his life among us was named Jesus. He not only created the vast universe which we inhabit, but in him "all things hold together" (Col. 1:17). To the human engineering feats that constructed the pyramids of Egypt, the aqueducts of Rome, the dikes that protect the Lowlands against the sea, the skyscrapers of New York, and the aeronautical genius that propelled men to the moon is now added the unwonted term "genetic engineering."

With none of these areas, however, was the Son of God, the Master Mind of the unimaginable achievements of the Creator, concerned during the days of his flesh. He did not give himself to the contemplation and execution of what we generally think of as "great achievements." On the contrary, he gave himself to doing lowly and humble things, to cultivating values little esteemed by the generality of mankind. Therefore, the engineering competence of the Creator was overshadowed by the healing service of the Redeemer, for he was concerned with this:

> Come to me, all who labor and are heavy laden, and I will give you rest. Take my yoke upon you, and learn from me; for I am gentle and lowly in heart, and you will find rest for your souls. For my yoke is easy, and my burden is light. (Matt. 11:28-30)

In contemplating such things, Paul wrote to the Philippian Christians,

> Have this mind among yourselves, which is yours in Christ Jesus, who, though he was in the form of God, did not count equality with God a thing to be grasped, but emptied himself, taking the form of a servant, being born in the likeness of men. And being found in human form he humbled himself and became obedient unto death, even death on a cross. (Phil. 2:5-8)

The writer of the letter to the Hebrews declares that in these last days God has spoken to us by a Son through whom he has created all things, a Son who "reflects the glory of God and bears the very stamp of his nature [the *imago Dei*], upholding the universe by his word of power" (1:1-3). Why did the one who is the image of God preeminently and our example in all things not perform the creationally ordained works of the image-bearer of God? When Jesus had an unparalleled opportunity to become king of Israel on his own terms (Matt. 21:1-13), and in that capacity initiate a model form of government and administrative service, why didn't he take it?

This question is the more pertinent because many followers of Jesus, especially those with Reformed antecedents, consider Christian involvement in the life of neighborhood and nation a high priority. They believe that they have been redeemed to do Christianly and in ever-expanding depth the tasks laid upon our first parents. Indeed, it is an innate human urge to be master and lord of all we can touch in time and space. The fall into sin did not deprive Man of his stewardship of all things put under his care, nor of joy and vigor in executing it. It radically altered the orientation of the stewardship responsibility, but it did not withdraw or cancel the given task of God's vicegerent on earth. Man remained, however brokenly, *imago Dei.*

Why did Jesus not point the way to the service of God and man in a showcase of governmental administration? Or, if not there, in some other area of human endeavor or human need?

Let us consider the problem to which Jesus as the incarnate Son of God addressed himself. It was to get humanity back to where it had been before the fall into sin. We have said that Man's condition before the fall was existence in a condition of integrity and wholeness in the four basic relationships in which God had created him—to God, to his neighbor, to the world, and to himself—in the recognition that the vertical relationship to God in holiness and obedience decisively determines the horizontal relationships in holiness and love to the neighbor, to the world, and to oneself. In short, the work of Jesus was to effect the return of mankind to the structure of existence in integrity, into which it had been introduced by the fact of creation.

That God resorted to sending his Son to effect this restoration is evidence enough that there was no built-in remedy for sin in the created universe. So far as creation is concerned, God assumed that its goodness (Gen. 1:31) would never be undone. When it was undone, a remedy was required that sustained no relationship to resources inherent in the existing world. The world as created provided no bridge between itself and its redemption.

Reformed theology has largely ignored this. It has been able to do so without theological discomfort by means of its concept of the eternal counsel of God. Redemption in Reformed theology is just as much a part of God's plan for the universe as creation is. There is no hint of an ad hoc resort on God's part to incarnation to save his creation. Reformed theology has transformed God's word to the serpent (not to Adam and Eve)—"I will put enmity between you and the woman, and between your seed and her seed; he shall bruise your head, and you shall bruise his heel" (Gen. 3:15)—into a clear statement of the essentials of the gospel. There is hardly a break between the state of rectitude and the state of sin. Before Adam and Eve leave the garden of Eden, the plan of their redemption is in place.

With the help of the Platonic conception of Being, Augustine transformed the dynamic God of time and movement of the Old and the New Testaments into a God for whom there is neither past nor future. Whatever was, is, or will be exists for him in an all-encompassing present which knows no duration. There is therefore really no disjunction between creation and redemption. Redemption through the work of the second Adam was waiting in the wings to enter the stage of the divine-human drama. Even that statement, so far as it relates to God's understanding, is, from an Augustinian point of view, an intolerable concession to the biblical conception of God's relationship to history.

There is, of course, both a thoroughly organic and a thoroughly biblical point of connection between creation and redemption. But it is not native to creation. It is our Lord Jesus Christ, who through God's special provision was born of Mary and as such is descended from the first Adam. He was born in the Palestinian village of Bethlehem, "born of woman, born under the law" (Gal. 4:4). He did not come as some alien from outer space; "he came to his own home," and though he was not welcome there, it was nevertheless "his own people" who did not receive him (John 1:11).

In Christ the two pillars of creation and redemption, nature and grace, stand together as the enduring foundation of both an effective salvation and a biblical theology about it. In him the Creator and the Redeemer meet to effect the redemption of mankind, of the world, and of the universe. In him the *imago Dei* finds its highest, noblest, and most efficacious expression.

We must look more directly at why Jesus did not become a great engineer or, for that matter, some other kind of famed achiever in the kingdom of God. We have noted that the purpose of the incarnation of our Lord was to restore the integrity of the four great relations in which he himself existed in the world, namely, to God, to his neighbor, to the environing world, and to himself.

The alienation into which the fall plunged us is called death; the reconciliation which Christ effected is called life. The Bestower of this life is God in Christ.

The impartation of this life was the sole purpose of God's coming to us in Christ. His life and ministry, his death and resurrection provided the unshakeable foundation for the coming of the Holy Spirit of life at Pentecost. Through the preaching of the gospel and its acceptance by faith, the four cornerstone human relationships undergo radical reorientation: vertically to their true center in God, horizontally to their true expression in integrity. Basically, in terms of the theme of this book, the work of Christ was and remains the restoration of the marred and disoriented *imago Dei* to its creationally given soundness and beauty.

This rehabilitation of mankind was in the view of God and of his Christ so basic that the effectuation of mere improvement in the lot of mankind in one or another area of life had to be subordinated to it. Reconciliation to God is the *sine qua non* of all the others.

That is why Jesus in pursuing his earthly course never became more than a simple rabbi who uncompromisingly hewed to the line of his calling. He had a baptism to be baptized with, and how constrained he was until it should be accomplished (Luke 12:50).

For his name was not simply Jesus, the son of Joseph and Mary. He knew himself to be the Christ, that is, the Messiah, the anointed one. He was anointed to be prophet, priest, and king, the climactic realization in one person of the triple office that had grown in Israel after Abraham's call to be the father of a separate people. And this separate people was at the same time, however paradoxically, a representative universal people.

His lineage, which in the Gospel of Matthew is wholly Jewish, begins: "The book of the genealogy of Jesus Christ, the son of David, the son of Abraham" (1:1). The more universally minded Luke traces it back to "Adam, the son of God" (3:38). But even Matthew does not understand Abraham's function to be restrictive. He reports that John the Baptist rebuked the Pharisees and Sadducees for religious nationalism: "Do not presume to say to yourselves, 'We have Abraham as our father'; for I tell you, God is able from these stones to raise up children to Abraham"

(3:7-9). Jesus held high the Roman centurion, saying of him, "not even in Israel have I found such faith. I tell you, many will come from east and west and sit at table with Abraham, Isaac, and Jacob in the kingdom of heaven" (Matt. 8:5-13). And Jesus' command to evangelize the nations finds its fullest expression in Matthew's well-known Great Commission (28:18-20).

It is Paul, however, who in his letter to the Romans gives the greatest depth to Israel's universal reference. He embraced Abraham as Israel's father. What is it that distinguished Abraham? It was his faith. When did Abraham believe? When he was still Abram, that is to say, while he was one of the common mass of Aramean people undistinguished by the rite of circumcision. What does this say about his faith? It says that he did not believe as a Jew, nor as an Israelite, but simply as a human being who belonged to the Aramean family of peoples.

> He received circumcision as a sign or seal of the righteousness which he had by faith while he was still uncircumcised. The purpose was to make him the father of all who believe without being circumcised and who thus have righteousness reckoned to them, and likewise the father of the circumcised who are not merely circumcised but also follow the example of the faith which our father Abraham had before he was circumcised. (Rom. 4:11-12)

In Paul's judgment, therefore, as in Jesus' own, Abraham transcended the insularity into which Israel had sunk. The faith that distinguished Abraham (and ideally all his physical descendants) he had held *before* his circumcision; thus he held it not as the "Jewish" Abraham but as the Gentile Aramean Abram. His new name "Abraham" meant "father of a multitude" and through later prophecy came to signify "many nations."

That is to say, the calling of Abram did not undo but rather affirmed God's concern for the human race as a whole, for the fact of circumcision *after* the event of Abram's faith shows that faith is fundamentally a reality *within* the context of humanity as a whole. Of this Melchizedek remained an abiding symbol.

Paul's argument shows that the long hiatus between Babel

and Pentecost was an apparent but not a real lapse in the continuity of God's involvement, also redemptively, in the life of universal Man. His concern *centered* in Israel. But around that center God in sundry ways sustained and nourished the essential *imago* of himself in the nations that were not Israel.

Israel served as a severely reduced but nevertheless representative humanity within which God prepared his effective coming to mankind in Christ. When the right moment, the *kairos,* came, God overlooked "the times of ignorance . . . but now he commands all men everywhere to repent, because he has fixed a day on which he will judge the world in righteousness by a man whom he has appointed" (Acts 17:30-31).

Furthermore, so universal is the outreach of God in Christ that Paul reinstitutes the Adam figure in the person of Christ. Abraham is the father of Israel, but Adam is the father of mankind.

> For as by a man came death, by a man has come also the resurrection of the dead. For as in Adam all die, so also in Christ shall all be made alive. . . . "The first man Adam became a living being"; the last Adam became a life-giving spirit. . . .The first man was from the earth, a man of dust; the second man is from heaven. (1 Cor. 15:21-22, 45, 47; see also Rom. 5:12-21)

In short, what the first Adam destroyed—the fourfold right relationship to God, to the neighbor, to the world, and to himself—the second Adam restored in its integrity. This has, however, a deeper, ultimate meaning. In Christ Man is restored to his true self, that is, to being again the true and full image of God. "Just as we have borne the image of the man of dust, we shall also bear the image of the man of heaven" (1 Cor. 15:49). The redemption of mankind is the redemption of the *imago Dei.*

In this redeemed humanity the believer *participates* in the same manner in which every human being participates in the image of God in which Adam was created. As we have all been created in Adam, so we are created anew in Christ, who is the image of God in the new creation. We become members of his body, the church, which, so far as humanity is concerned, is the new creation. As such we participate in all the fullness of Christ, who in all his splendor, glory, and power is the image of God, bearing the very stamp of God's nature and upholding the universe by his word of power (Heb. 1:3). We are therefore not renewed after the image in which the first Adam was created. We are renewed after the image of the last Adam.

As we participate in Christ the image of God, so we also participate in his election:

> For those whom he foreknew he also predestined to be conformed to the image of his Son, in order that he might be the first-born among many brethren. (Rom. 8:29)

That Christ is here called "the first-born among many brethren" indicates clearly that we are conformed not simply to the Christ of creation, but to that Christ enriched by all his work and merit as the Christ of redemption. God has not only chosen us in him before the foundation of the world (Eph. 1:4), but has put all things under the feet of Christ and has made him head over all things for the church (Eph. 1:22). Thus creation and redemption embrace the same cosmic entity; *imago Dei,* election, and the church embrace the same human entity.

This composite, unitary, undivided work of Christ loses its wholeness and integrated character in the way Reformed theology has developed its understanding of redemption. A restraint has been placed upon the freedom of the Reformed theologian to think God's thoughts after him. This restraint is caused by Reformed theology's earlier noted Achilles' heel, namely, the doctrine of predestination, which splits the image of God into two eternally irreconcilable parts. True, the doctrine of reprobation has been by and large abandoned, eliminating a significant and illegitimate factor in theological reflection. But the continuation of individual election in the theological process leaves the hardly less foreboding factor of "the non-elect" to be taken into account.

Even if the historic Reformed confessions no longer play

the authoritative and normative role in the life of evangelical Presbyterian, Reformed, Congregational, and many Baptist churches which they did from the sixteenth to the nineteenth and even into the twentieth century, this does not mean that their momentum has been altogether spent. The discontinuation of their authority does not immediately clear the individual or collective mind of attitudes and perceptions they inculcated, particularly when such ideas are characterized by complexity and depth.

The Reformed doctrine of predestination did not merely split the numerical mass of individual human beings into two absolutely disparate parts. It bifurcated the human *race,* dividing the *imago Dei* into two eternally irreconcilable segments: the elect and the reprobate. Moreover, and even more importantly, this division was seen as essential to the proper glorification of God. Election exalted the *mercy* of God, reprobation his *justice.* This was not just a theory propounded by this or that theologian. It was inscribed and given ecclesiastical weight in major creeds of the sixteenth and seventeenth centuries:

> We believe that . . . God . . . calleth those whom he hath chosen . . . *to display in them the riches of his mercy;* leaving the rest in this same corruption and condemnation to *display in them his justice.* (French Confession, 1559, Art. 12)

> We believe that God . . . did then manifest Himself such as He is . . . : *merciful,* since he delivers . . . all whom He . . . has elected in Christ Jesus our Lord; . . . *just,* in leaving others in the fall and perdition wherein they have involved themselves. (Belgic Confession, 1561, Art. 16)

> For all things being ordained for the manifestation of his glory . . . being to appear both in the works of his *mercy* and of his *justice,* it seemed good to his heavenly wisdom to choose out a certain number toward whom he would extend his undeserved *mercy,* leaving the rest to be the *spectacles of his justice.* (Irish Articles of Religion, 1615, Par. 14)

> This elect number . . . God has decreed to give to Christ . . . and . . . finally to glorify them for the *demonstration of his mercy.* (Canons of Dort, 1618-19, I.7)

> Not all but some only are elected, while others are passed by whom . . . God . . . has decreed to leave in the common misery *for the declaration of his justice* to condemn and punish them forever. (Canons of Dort, 1618-19, I.15)

> Those of mankind that are predestinated unto life, God . . . hath chosen in Christ . . . and all to the *praise of his glorious grace.* (Westminster Confession, 1647, III.5)

> The rest of mankind God was pleased . . . to pass by, and to ordain them to dishonor and wrath for their sin, *to the praise of his glorious justice.* (Westminster Confession, 1647, III.7).

Presumably, the elect saints not only constitute an objective evidence of God's mercy but also consciously witness to it. The reprobate constitute objective evidence of God's justice and may therefore appropriately be called a "spectacle" of it. Conceivably, they themselves also, however reluctantly, testify to it.

On such a basis the reprobate are not only destined to be lost, but constitute *a necessary element* for the glorification of one of God's two putatively most essential qualities, namely justice. Thus the *whole* of the *imago Dei* in its eternally split-up form, the elect in heaven and the reprobate in hell, eternally testify to what God is alleged essentially to be, that is, merciful and just. In eternity, hell is as functional and indispensable for God's glory as heaven.

The Reformed churches of Dutch provenance long held this view of predestination, set forth notably in the Belgic Confession and the Canons of Dort. It was taught in catechetical classes, proclaimed from the pulpit, and elaborated on in religious literature for the laity, though always with the accent on election. Reprobation was in a minor key—not only because the subject was highly unpleasant but because the instruction in and proclamation of election effectively kept reprobation in the communal consciousness without talking about it.

In the course of the years there arose alongside this doctrine a teaching concerning an "antithesis" between "the church and the world." While an antithesis truly exists, it came too often to be held in the form of two fairly constant entities standing in opposition to each other, rather than as the church reaching out redemptively to reclaim the world for God. Fear and social and religious distance more than outreach and witness came to characterize the church's attitude to the unbelieving community. The rise of a strong movement for instituting separate Christian educational institutions strengthened the effect of the antithesis mentality in the Reformed community. The real danger, of course, was not Christian education, but uncritical acceptance and support of it in the context of antithetical thinking.

I cannot help feeling that there is a profound subconscious connection between the historic doctrine of predestination and the rise of the antithesis idea on the one hand and many Reformed people's inability to engage in one-on-one witness to Christ in neighborhood or marketplace on the other. Predestination is a doctrine which, while not disowned in most Reformed churches, is now relegated to a wholly secondary or tertiary role. But the attitudes and inhibitions it has nourished over the years cannot be disposed of as readily as can the doctrinal structures out of which they grew. Indeed, even the doctrinal structures are not really disposed of. They are just ignored.

It is encouraging to note how at the beginning of this century so unsurpassed a Reformed theologian as Herman Bavinck distanced himself from the election-mercy/reprobation-justice motif of these post-Reformation creeds. His disapproval of it bordered on censure. It is "all too simplistic and meagre,"[1] he writes, to say that in the eternal state God reveals his righteousness exclusively in those who are lost and his mercy exclusively in the elect. His righteousness is also revealed in the church, which was purchased by the blood of his Son; and even in the realm of destruction there are gradations of punishment and therefore glimmerings of mercy.

1. Bavinck, *Gereformeerde Dogmatiek,* 2:408.

In a remarkable paragraph Bavinck, in spite of his subscription to the election-reprobation schema, sets forth God's realization of the purpose of creation and redemption in terms of a restored *humanity* at the head of the restored cosmos:

> The focus of election is not on individual people, as is the case in reprobation. It is on the restoration of humanity, under a new Head, i.e., Christ. Grace saves the human race together with the entire cosmos. In this preservation of mankind and of the world God does not merely reveal some particular virtues, so that alongside of them an eternal destruction would be necessary to reveal his righteousness. Rather it is in the consummation of the kingdom of God that all his virtues and perfections will be displayed: his righteousness and his grace, his holiness and his love, his sovereignty and his mercy. It is this state of glory that God, albeit subject to his own honor, envisioned as the direct, the actual purpose of the creation of the universe.[2]

The idea that it is *mankind* that is saved by the work of Christ finds strong support in a recent book by Neal Punt entitled *Unconditional Good News: Toward an Understanding of Biblical Universalism.*[3] Punt appropriates a thesis propounded by Charles Hodge: "All the descendants of Adam, except those of whom it is expressly revealed that they cannot inherit the kingdom of God, are saved."[4] The immediate scriptural basis for this view Hodge finds in Romans 5:18:

> Then as one man's trespass led to condemnation for all men, so one man's act of righteousness leads to acquittal and life for all men.

For Punt this means that "all [persons] are saved or are elect in Christ except those the Bible declares will be lost."[5] This con-

2. Bavinck, *Gereformeerde Dogmatiek,* 2:406.

3. Neal Punt, *Unconditional Good News: Toward an Understanding of Biblical Universalism* (Grand Rapids: Eerdmans, 1980).

4. Charles Hodge, *Systematic Theology*, 3 vols. (Grand Rapids: Eerdmans, 1952), 1:26.

5. Punt, p. 4.

trasts rather sharply with the traditional understanding that "all [persons] are outside of Christ except those who the Bible declares will be saved."[6] The new formulation is not intended to be construed absolutely. It is a working principle, and as such it can have substantial Christian value. It makes it possible

> to view all persons and to treat them as those for whom Christ died, unless and until they give evidence to the contrary. On this basis we are to love all people, share with them the good news of what Christ has done for us.[7]

The exceptive clause here ("unless. . . ") constitutes a problem to which we shall return.

Punt also comments at some length on what we have been calling the "split" in the *imago Dei.* He speaks of it in terms of two "camps." He believes in a single unitary group of the elect only, which in his view constitutes all mankind. This, too, of course, is a working principle to which there are exceptions. Presumably the exceptions cannot be regarded as a valid, organic, unitary entity. They exist, but they do not have a right to existence. It is probably fair to refer to them as sickly fruit that has fallen from the tree of humanity, no longer considered as part of the family of Man.

The way in which Punt elaborates his thesis invites reservations, centering on the way he understands election. Punt embraces without qualification the Reformed teaching concerning election. He sets it forth scripturally and credally. The Belgic Confession, the Canons of Dort, and the Westminster Confession all make their contribution to his argument. He quotes Ephesians 2:8-9: "For by grace you have been saved through faith; and this is not your own doing, it is the gift of God—not because of works, lest any man should boast." The premise of biblical universalism "presupposes a definite number of elect."[8] The Canons of Dort teach "that the elect cannot be cast away, 'nor their number

6. Punt, p. 5.
7. Punt, p. 7.
8. Punt, p. 28.

diminished' (I, 11)"[9] and the Westminster Confession teaches similarly.

What Punt fails to take into theological account is that all these creeds explicitly treat election as one of two divisions under the more inclusive heading of predestination. The other division is reprobation. He observes that if one accepts "as an axiom . . . an eternal election to salvation or a definite number of elect or a fixed decree," reason compels acceptance of a "two-camp" view of predestination.[10] This is wholly correct. If there is a definite number of elect which does not include all mankind person for person, there is no way to deny that there must be what the Canons call "non-elect" or, more definitely, "the reprobate."

But Punt does not agree with this reasoning. We should "not permit our understanding of reason to conclude that [God's] rejection of some is the inevitable consequence of definite, eternal, particular election of individuals to salvation." But he must inescapably do something about those who are not elected. This indeed he does—in a very novel manner. It is more accurate, he writes, "to speak of predestination or eternal election in terms of one camp of persons surrounded by 'no man's land.'"[11] It is "no man's land" because "no one has a right to be outside of Christ"; those outside of him "can blame no one other than themselves for being there." No one "remains there against his own will"; no one on earth "is hopelessly and helplessly consigned there." The Bible "speaks of this 'no man's land' as an inexplicable darkness, as 'the mystery of lawlessness.'"[12]

This is all well said, but it does not address the point that both election and reprobation speak to in the historic Reformed creeds to which Punt appeals. The Reformed doctrine of predestination, while certainly not devoid of historical significance, is basically a doctrine of eternal import. It is futuristic in its ultimate mean-

9. Punt, p. 71.
10. Punt, pp. 58-59.
11. Punt, p. 59.
12. Punt, p. 59.

ing, and that future does not lie in this life, but in the eternal life to come. The personal judgment of a theologian cannot hold to one half of the predestination doctrine and simply brush the other aside. So much is reprobation an inseparable companion doctrine of election that in the post-Reformation creeds God's receiving the eternal glory due him depends as much on it as on election.[13] The two constitute an inseparable and indissoluble union of ultimate opposites, which bears the name Predestination.

The inseparableness of election and reprobation in Reformed theology is further evidenced by their powerful common root in *the sovereign good pleasure of God.* The elect are not elect because they believed. The reprobate are not rejected because they disbelieved. Concerning reprobation the Canons of Dort say this:

> Others are passed by in the eternal decree; whom God, out of his sovereign, most just, irreprehensible and unchangeable good pleasure, has decreed to leave in the common misery into which they have wilfully plunged themselves, and not to bestow upon them saving faith and the grace of conversion; but, permitting them in his just judgment to follow their own ways, at last, for the declaration of his justice to condemn and punish them forever, not only on account of their unbelief, but also for all their other sins. (I.15)

The Canons, whatever one may think of them, are a masterpiece of logical unity. Reprobation is infrequently stated, but it is as basic to their structure as election. Reprobation limits election; *therefore,* the Canons teach *limited atonement.* Election cannot be changed or altered; *therefore* there is *perseverance of the saints.* Salvation is by grace alone; *therefore,* both election *and* reprobation are the result of God's *sovereign good pleasure.*

The Canons of Dort constitute one indivisible piece. It is not theologically possible to take election as it stands there as the effective cause of salvation and wholly disregard the fully parallel declaration in I.15 that God "*decreed* . . . not to bestow upon them [the reprobate] saving faith and the grace of conversion."

13. See also pp. 161 and 162 above.

The elect are not chosen because of their faith, and the rejected are not cast away because of their unbelief. God's sovereign good pleasure is the full and exclusive cause of *both* election *and* reprobation in the historical Reformed credal and theological tradition.

For this reason, the second clause of Punt's declaration that "Salvation is by grace; damnation is by works"[14] is untenable. True, on the great day of judgment the saints will be rewarded for their faithfulness and obedience, and unbelievers will be punished for their disobedience and rejection of salvation. But this in no way makes either obedience or disobedience the ground of God's ultimate judgment on the lives of men. The ground for election is God's sovereign will, and so is the ground for reprobation. It is the will of God not to bestow on the reprobate "saving faith and the grace of conversion." For this decision no rationale is given, and it is an act of human pride to seek to divine it. All the convolutions and involutions of Reformed theology to soften or blur or mitigate this judgment are but evidences of deep and painful embarrassment.

All of this must not lead us to close our eyes to the merits of Punt's effort to make a crucial point of Reformed theology both more biblical and more humane. His significant contribution, which no criticism can dim, is his repudiation of two-camp predestination theology and his specific rejection of reprobation. This helps to clear the ground for what we must turn to next and finally, namely, the manner in which we are to understand a structure of individual election which is not part of a complex that requires consideration of the human entity known as "reprobate" or "non-elect." The several considerations brought forward in this chapter make it all the more relevant to seek to formulate biblically a structure of election which is not part of a complex that requires consideration of a human entity known as the reprobate or the non-elect. With that we will conclude the argument of this book.

14. Punt, p. 24.

Chapter X

Elect in Christ

He chose us in him before the foundation of the world. . . . He destined us in love to be his sons through Jesus Christ.

Ephesians 1:4-5

It is striking that Reformed credal theology in its classic expression has as its centerpiece the doctrine of predestination, with its dual election-reprobation character, a doctrine concerned exclusively with the eternal fate of individual human beings. This centrality of predestination thus understood is peculiar for three reasons.

First, as we have emphasized, God's dealings with mankind, in both creation and redemption, are with the whole of humanity. Through creation God brought into being the race of mankind. In seeking to redeem fallen Man, he dealt directly with the whole of humanity from the fall to the flood, and again from the flood to the dispersion of mankind through the confusion of tongues at Babel.

Second, the calling of Abraham to become the father of a separate people did not constitute a break in the divine redemptive strategy. Rather, it intensified it. In Abraham and through his descendants "all the families of the earth" would be blessed

(Gen. 12:3). Israel became God's "first-born son" (Ex. 4:22), the representative symbol of the new humanity which the work of Christ would bring into being. The Bible teaches three distinct elective acts of God which together embrace the entirety of the redemptive process: the election of Israel, the election of Christ, and the election of the church.

In the third place, none of these elections has a reprobatory counter-aspect. There is no reprobate Israel, there is no reprobate Christ, and there is no reprobate church. "Reprobate" here does not mean an apostate, heretical, false, or backsliding human entity which became such in the course of history. It means reprobation in the sense of an eternal decree of God which formally has the same source and force and duration as God's elective decree of individuals. In the doctrine of predestination, election and reprobation are antithetical companion acts of God with respect to the salvation and nonsalvation of individual human beings.

For these reasons the doctrine of predestination may be seen as seriously undercutting a massive motif in the history of creation and redemption as set forth in the Scriptures. That motif is God's carrying out his deepest intentions with Man, whether creationally or redemptively, in terms of mankind as a whole, that is, in terms of his *imago,* his *entire* image, not in terms of what we described in the preceding chapter as a split in it.

We can understand how the doctrine of election might be thrown off course from a unitary conception of mankind to a split view of it. The fact is that the Bible often speaks of "elect" people as the obedient, the devout in distinction from the unbelieving, that is, the unrepentant. God says in Isaiah, "for like the days of a tree shall the days of my people be, and my chosen shall long enjoy the work of their hands" (65:22). For the sake of the elect the tribulation of the end-time shall be shortened (Matt. 24:22). After the tribulation the Son of Man shall gather his elect from the four winds (Mark 13:27). Paul endures all things for the sake of the elect (2 Tim. 2:10). Paul's apostolic task is to further the faith of God's elect (Titus 1:1). Who shall lay anything to the charge of God's elect? (Rom. 8:33).

These and similar passages must, however, be seen in the larger context of the relation of the elect to the elect Christ. To this we now turn.

This book is written on the assumption that the *imago Dei* does not consist of millions and billions of human images of God. It sees *humanity,* the sum total of all human beings, mutually related in a unitary organic entity as the image of God. In that vast fullness each human being in the world participates. It is that participation which makes persons human and distinguishes them from the animal kingdom. Through natural generation the image of God that was Adam and Eve was enlarged on and on until it filled the earth.

When we read those passages in the New Testament that speak of Christ as image of God, it may seem that he is by and in himself and without reference to progeny the *imago Dei.* At first glance he may seem to be a singular divine being who, when his identity is recognized, is seen to fully reflect the Godhead: "He who has seen me has seen the Father" (John 14:9); he came to dwell among us, full of grace and truth, and "we have beheld his glory, glory as of the only Son from the Father" (John 1:14); Christ is the likeness of God (2 Cor. 4:4); he is "the image of the invisible God" (Col. 1:15); he "reflects the glory of God and bears the very stamp of his nature" (Heb. 1:3).

If these citations are adduced without reference to context, the similarity of Christ to progeny-producing Adam as image of God is obscured by the absence of a clear-cut, immediate definition of what it means to be image of God as in the case of Adam and Eve: "So God created man in his own image, in the image of God he created him; male and female he created them. And God blessed them, and said to them, 'Be fruitful and multiply, and fill the earth and subdue it; and have dominion'" (Gen. 1:27-28).

In fact, however, when we consider other relevant data of Scripture, the similarity between the *imago* of creation and the *imago* of redemption as it relates to Christ is astounding. As Adam was the organic head of the human race, first in its integrity and then in its fallen state, so is Christ the organic head of the human race as reclaimed, of which the church is the representative reality.

I use the word *organic* here advisedly. The noun form of the adjective *organic* is *organism.* What is an organism? Webster's *New Collegiate Dictionary* describes it as "an individual constituted to carry on the activities of life by means of organs separate in function but mutually dependent: a living being." It is in this sense that the position of Christ in the economy of salvation is that of a head in relation to its body. He in whom all things were created, who is before all things and in whom "all things hold together," is in the full significance of the word *organism* "the head of the body, the church" (Col. 1:16-18). He fully informs and indwells the church; and the body in its several organs fully finds its life and rationale and purpose in him as its head. The significance of this figure must be pursued further as a basis for understanding the election of believers in Christ *without* a corresponding reprobatory rejection.

The New Testament sets forth this relationship in many ways. Christ is the true vine, and we are the branches. When we abide in him and he in us, we bear much fruit; and without him we can do nothing (John 15:1-5). He is "the first-born among many brethren" (Rom. 8:29); he is "the first-born of all creation" (Col. 1:15). "Just as we have borne the image of the man of dust, we shall also bear the image of the man of heaven" (1 Cor. 15:49). He is the Good Shepherd, who lays down his life for the sheep; he knows his own, and his own know him; he is also the door through which the sheep enter the sheepfold (John 10:9, 11, 14).

These representative passages from the New Testament are climaxed in a brief but constantly recurring and eminently telling expression in the writings of St. Paul: "in Christ" or "in him." These words sum up the intimacy and depth of the relationship between Christ the head and believers in him both collectively as a body, the church, and individually as members of the body. Paul became the father of the Corinthian Christians *in Christ Jesus* through the gospel (1 Cor. 4:15); he sent Timothy, his beloved and faithful child *in the Lord,* to the

Corinthians to remind them of his ways *in Christ* (4:17); as in Adam all die, so *in Christ* shall all be made alive (15:22). *In Christ* God leads us in triumph (2 Cor. 2:14); *in Christ* we are a new creation (5:17); *in Christ Jesus* we have freedom (Gal. 2:4); we are all one *in Christ Jesus* (3:28). For our sake God made him to be sin who knew no sin, so that *in him* we might become the righteousness of God (2 Cor. 5:21); we have been raised and made to sit with him in the heavenly places *in Christ Jesus* (Eph. 2:6); Paul enjoins Timothy to follow his words in the faith and love which are *in Christ Jesus* (2 Tim. 1:13) and to be strong in the grace that is *in Christ Jesus* (2:1); the Gentiles are partakers of the promise *in Christ Jesus* through the gospel (Eph. 3:6). Nothing is able to separate us from the love of God *in Christ Jesus our Lord* (Rom. 8:39).

Were we to choose one word that most aptly characterizes the activity of believers in the appropriation of all that Christ gives to men, it would be the word *participation*. Our relation to Christ in the dispensation of grace is the same as our participation in the humanity of Adam in the state of integrity and subsequently in the state of sin. By birth we participate in the life of Adam and by rebirth in the life of Christ. Romans 5:15-21 is decisive here: "Then as one man's trespass led to condemnation for all men, so one man's act of righteousness leads to acquittal and life for all men" (v. 18).

Whether fallen or redeemed, the human race moves as a unit through all the stages of its existence. It was created as a unit; it fell as a unit; it is being redeemed as a unit. Herman Bavinck shows a large and perceptive vision of this truth in writing,

> The object of election is not simply a number of individual people, as is the case in reprobation. In election it is the human race under a new head, namely Christ, that is its object. Therefore it is not merely individuals that are saved by grace, but the human race as such along with the entirety of the redeemed cosmos.[1]

1. Bavinck, *Gereformeerde Dogmatiek*, 2:406.

The race as an organic unit, therefore, is saved. The reprobate by God's decree become separate unrelated individuals without a naturally given cohesiveness, like leaves that fall from the tree at the approach of winter. But the towering tree of humanity remains, its integrity untouched. In the matter of reprobation Bavinck remained a son of his tradition. His assent to it surfaces in various places, though usually in low key, sometimes even critically. Even so, his vision was large and rich within the limiting framework of predestination and invites fuller development apart from that framework.

It is therefore strange that, in contrast with this tremendous weight of organically interrelated humanity, whether as fallen in the first Adam or as redeemed in the last Adam, the Reformed tradition as a whole presents us with "a certain number of persons" (Canons of Dort, I.7) elected for redemption in Christ, which election "can neither be interrupted nor changed, recalled or annulled . . . nor their number diminished" (I.11). The Westminster Confession is no less clear: the number of those who are predestinated whether to life or to death "is so certain and definite, that it cannot be increased or diminished" (III.iv). The contrast is between "numbers" in predestination theology and humanity as a whole in the threefold scriptural teaching of election.

In the historic Reformed view, the elect apparently bear no natural relationship to each other. True, in history they come to constitute the church, the body of Christ, but for all that, its constituent members are a group of separate individuals, that is, a number, chosen by God before they existed for reasons unrelated to their religious or moral worth. They are elect by reason of God's "sovereign good pleasure," the rationale of which he has not revealed. Its counterpart is the horrible reality of the reprobate, to which they were destined from times eternal by the same rationale that gives eternal bliss to the elect. With Paul we must say to that aspect of the Reformed tradition, "You did not so learn Christ!" (Eph. 4:20).

What is needed therefore is a doctrine of election which does not stand in the traditional election-reprobation framework of

Reformed theology. This is needed because the Bible is clear not only on the election of Israel, Christ, and the church, but also on the election of individuals. By these individuals I do not have in mind elect kings and prophets in Israel or elect apostles and bishops of the church, but elect members of the community of Israel and elect members of the body of Christ. This is, however, a derived election, discovered in time, which is not burdened by a corresponding reprobation, and is therefore akin to the triple election of Israel, Christ, and the church. Of this distinctive kind of personal election we must first take note.

The scripturally impermissible conjunction of election and reprobation must be replaced by the scripturally warranted and pastorally illuminating and comforting conjunction of election and *participation.* This participation is the believers' sharing in Christ, who is the head of the new humanity. As we were created in the life of the first Adam, so are we recreated in the life of the second Adam. As we participated in the unmarred humanity of Adam, which was lost, so we participate in the election of Christ as the head of the new humanity, which cannot be lost. Through faith in Christ we become part of his body, the church; through faith we become part of the new humanity; through faith we share in his election.[2]

It is, of course, thoroughly impermissible in historic Reformed theology to suggest that we "become" elect in Christ. It is quite appropriate to say that in Christ we become a new creation, that by conversion and faith we become believers, that in him we participate in the communion of saints. But election, according to the tradition, is *from eternity.* One cannot become what one already is. The believer does become *aware* in time of his or her election, but in no way can he or she *become* elect in Christ in history.

2. In his book *The Freedom of God: A Study of Election and Pulpit* (Grand Rapids: Eerdmans, 1973), James Daane has a remarkable section on the believer's participation in Christ's anointing, which he understands to be synonymous with Christ's election. Cf. pp. 197-201.

How valid is this Reformed view? Several considerations must be taken into account here.

The spiritual strength that made individual Israelites to be Israelites indeed was the consciousness instilled into them from childhood that they were members of an elect nation. It was not a sense of personal election by God that moved them in the depths of their soul. It was rather the collective awareness that they were a people distinct from all other nations on the earth. They were a nation "chosen by God" to play a role given to no other people. In God's name Moses told the king of one of the great empires of antiquity, "Israel is my first-born son" (Exod. 4:22); and no Israelite ever forgot this. The pious among them heard with humility and reverence God's rebuke through Amos, "You only have I known of all the families of the earth; therefore I will punish you for all your iniquities" (3:2). Spiritual riches led to spiritual pride, and secular nationalism replaced devout religion. But whether it was one or the other, the strength of the individual lay in being a member of the body of the nation, not in a sense of personal divine election. His or her pride and joy in life lay in complete identification with the larger self—the elect people of God. Self-realization lay in participation in the community of Israel, the elect nation.

The theme of Israel as the elect nation carried over into the intertestamental period. We may cite some examples from the apocryphal writings that flourished between 200 B.C. and A.D. 100.

> Joshua the son of Nun . . . became, in accordance with his name, a great savior of God's elect . . . so that he might give Israel its inheritance. (Ecclesiasticus 46:1)

> Those who trust in him will understand truth . . . because grace and mercy are upon his elect, and he watches over his holy ones. (Wisdom of Solomon 3:9-10)

> "Behold," says God, "I call together all the kings of the earth. . . . Just as they have done to my elect until this day, so I will do, and will repay into their bosom." (2 Esdras 15:20-21)

> For they [the wicked] shall destroy and plunder [the] goods [of the righteous], and drive them out of their houses. Then the tested quality of my elect shall be manifest, as gold that is tested by fire. "Hear, my elect," says the Lord. "Behold, the days of tribulation are at hand, and I will deliver you from them." (2 Esdras 16:72-74)

In these passages "the elect" refers either to the Jewish nation or to the devout in the Jewish nation. There is no indication here or elsewhere that "the elect" are referred to as individual persons who are taken up in an eternal decree of God and thus distinguished from the reprobate.

This sense of being an elect people, which grew in the Jewish nation over the centuries, was in time taken over by the Christian community and applied to its own relationship to God. In the New Testament the elect are seen not so much as an organized or institutional entity but as children of God, whether individually or collectively. In the parable of the importunate widow and the unrighteous judge, Jesus said, "And will not God vindicate his elect, who cry to him day and night?" (Luke 18:7). Paul wrote, "If God is for us, who is against us? . . . Who shall bring any charge against God's elect?" (Rom. 8:31, 33). In 2 Timothy 2:10, he wrote, "therefore I endure everything for the sake of the elect." And again, "Paul, a servant of God and an apostle of Jesus Christ, to further the faith of God's elect and their knowledge of the truth . . ." (Titus 1:1).

In all these passages "the elect" may as properly be called "believers," "people of God," or, as already in the earliest time of the church, "Christians." The use of the word *elect* simply signified the transformation of a deeply held Jewish conviction into an equally deeply felt Christian belief. It had religious but no significant theological reference. For this reason it would be hazardous to substantiate Reformed predestinarian theology with appeals to such passages.

According to G. Schrenk, the first epistle of Peter is the place in the New Testament where election begins to have theological structure. Writing in the *Theological Dictionary of the New Testament,* Schrenk notes that

> 1 Pt. is the only NT work in which ["elect"] has from the very outset thematic significance. . . . In 1:1 the readers are characterised . . . as [elect exiles of the Dispersion.] . . . The ref. is to Gentile Christians, who are figuratively aliens, living in dispersion here on earth. In this age their position is that of foreigners, but they belong to the company of the elect. They are [elect exiles], v. 2: [according to the foreknowledge of God the Father, in sanctification of the Spirit for obedience and sprinkling of the blood of Jesus Christ.] . . ."
>
> As may be seen from 2:11: [as sojourners and aliens], this opening theme is further developed in 2:4-10. The supremely important point here is that basic OT promises and predicates, which originally applied to the people of Israel, are now transferred to the universal Christian community. Christianity knows that it is the elect Israel. Christ is the chosen corner-stone of the temple. . . . Through Him the community becomes a temple, a priesthood offering sacrifices. . . . It is [an elect race], a holy people, a people of possession. The transfer is wholly grounded upon, and executed by, Christ. There can be little room for doubt that emphasis is here laid upon the link between the [chosen stone] (Christ) and the [chosen nation].[3]

In 1 Peter 2:7-8 the subject of election is continued. It begins with "To you therefore *who believe, he is precious,*" and then adds the antithetical "but for those who do not believe, 'The very stone which the builders rejected has become the head of the corner,' and '*A stone that will make men stumble, a rock that will make them fall'; for they stumble because they disobey the word, as they were destined to do.*" On this outstanding "reprobation passage" Schrenk comments:

> It is certainly not said that from all eternity the world has been divided into the predestined and the reprobate. What is said is that everything depends upon whether one is willing or not to believe in Christ and to obey Him. . . . It is illegitimate to extend the [as

3. G. Shrenk, "*Eklektos* in the New Testament," *Theological Dictionary of the New Testament,* ed. Gerhard Kittel, trans. Geoffrey W. Bromiley (Grand Rapids: Eerdmans, 1967), IV:190. Bracketed material is my translation of the Greek in the original.

> they were destined to do] of 2:8 to mean that they cannot do otherwise because hereto foreordained from all eternity.[4]

Linguistically and exegetically it is completely warranted to understand "as they were destined to do" to mean that their life was of such a nature as to lead to their self-destruction.

Is it so strange that believers should see themselves elect in Christ as the inevitable consequence of genuine faith? If they are buried with him in baptism, if they participate in his glory, if in the boldness of Peter's words they become through his power "partakers of the divine nature" (2 Pet. 1:4), is it not appropriate that they should participate in his election? For to participate in his election is to participate in that for which he came to earth as the elect of God.

The redemptive work of Christ has a core around which the whole of his ministry centered. It is the central core of *service.* The Son of Man did not come to be served but to serve, "and to give his life as a ransom for many" (Matt. 20:28). His food was to do the will of him who had sent him and to accomplish his work (John 4:34). These and many similar passages find their climax in Paul's letter to the Philippians:

> Have this mind among yourselves, which is yours in Christ Jesus, who, though he was in the form of God, did not count equality with God a thing to be grasped, but emptied himself, taking the form of a servant, being born in the likeness of men. And being found in human form he humbled himself and became obedient unto death, even death on a cross. (2:5-8)

If election is election to service as well as to salvation, it would seem fitting to regard it as a *participation* in the mission of Christ. We are fellow workers together with him (2 Cor. 6:1), in the common task. As his ambassadors (2 Cor. 5:20), we serve and speak for the king and his kingdom. It is to this fellowship in service that our faith appoints or calls us. It is in the pursuit of

4. Shrenk, p. 191.

this service that the believer is encouraged by the exhortation in 2 Peter 1:10—"make your calling and election sure," which a traditional Reformed theologian can only find embarrassing. How can we look into the eternal counsel of God to make sure our names are written in the book of life? We can, however, be diligent about knowing that as living members of the elect church of God we are standing and walking in the tradition of those who have gone before. Basically, the apostolic instruction means this: confirm your spiritual membership in the body of Christ by word and conduct becoming to a believer.

We may observe here that the Bible has little to say about "the number" of the elect. Isaiah illustrates this in the case of Israel. God's "chosen" shall inherit the promised land, and his servants shall dwell there (65:9), and his "chosen" shall long enjoy the work of their hands (v. 22). Here the elect are seen simply as the devout in the nation. The same is true in Matthew 24:31, where it is said that the angels shall gather God's elect from the four winds. In Luke 18:7 God assures the faithful that he will vindicate his own elect who cry to him day and night; in 2 Timothy 2:10 Paul writes that he endures everything "for the sake of the elect, that they also may obtain salvation in Christ Jesus."

Apparently, "she who is at Babylon, who is likewise chosen, sends you greetings" (1 Pet. 5:13) is a reference to the body of a local congregation in which, as of the entire church of Christ, probably not all were Israel that were of Israel (cf. Rom. 9:6).

Indeed, this is precisely the case in 2 John: "The elder to the elect lady and her children. . . . I rejoiced greatly to find some of your children following the truth" (vv. 1, 4). By almost common consent among New Testament interpreters, the "elect lady" is an unknown church or congregation which has a number of members, of whom "some" are faithful to the gospel. The "elect lady" also has an "elect sister" (v. 13), whose "children" send through John a greeting to the "elect lady."

The Reformed creed that encapsulates this theme most effectively is the Heidelberg Catechism. In answering the question

"What do you believe concerning the holy catholic Church?" the catechism says,

> That the Son of God, out of the whole human race, from the beginning to the end of the world, gathers, defends, and preserves for Himself, by his Spirit and Word, in the unity of the true faith, a Church chosen to everlasting life; and that I am, and forever shall remain, a living member thereof. (Q. and A. 54)

Here the object of God's elective grace is the church, the body of Christ, the new humanity, and therefore the renewed *imago Dei.* In this elect body believers *participate* because they are *members* of it. The Lord Jesus Christ is the last Adam, who through his Word and Spirit gives life to all who by faith share in his election.

The adjective "elect," therefore, has several meanings in the Old Testament, the New Testament, and the literature of the intertestamental period. It can refer to Israel, to Christ (the Messiah), to the church, to a remnant of the faithful, to a group of believers existing at a particular time or place, or to a congregation. Where the elect are referred to as a whole, it is much more natural in the context to understand them as faithful members of Israel or of the church than as objects of an individual election in eternity which has reprobation as its inevitable counterpart. As a noun, the use of the word *elect*, apart from Christ, always refers to, or derives from, its association with elect Israel or elect church. In short, a particular person in his or her own right, so to speak, is never referred to as "elect" in the Bible in the Reformed sense of individual election.

How are all these considerations related to the central concern of this book, the meaning of the *imago Dei* concept for Reformed theology?

In the course of Paul's great exposition of the relationship existing between Jews and Gentiles (Rom. 9–11), he sees both elect Israel and unbelieving Gentiles as playing profound roles in God's plan of redemption, which to our understanding can only be described as inscrutable and marvelous. Israel has rejected the gospel as it rejected the message of the prophets in the time of Isaiah: all day long God has held out his hand to a disobedient and contrary people (10:21). Has he then rejected his people? By no means. Is not Paul himself an Israelite, a member of the tribe of Benjamin? Was there not in the time of Elijah a faithful remnant? So, too, at the present time there is a remnant chosen by grace. But Israel as a whole was hardened. God gave them a spirit of stupor, eyes that should not see and ears that should not hear, down to Paul's very day (11:1-8).

Nevertheless, far from rejecting Israel, God used its disobedience for two kingdom-enriching developments. God sent the gospel to the Gentiles, who accepted it, and this had an effect on Israel. It made them jealous and in this manner prepared the way for their return to the ancestral faith. Then follows this amazing conclusion:

> Now if their trespass means riches for the world, and if their failure means riches for the Gentiles, how much more will their full inclusion mean! (11:12)

Unbelief and disobedience in Israel were instrumental in God's redemptive providence to further the ultimate aim of the inclusion of the Gentiles in the body of Christ.

Having established this, Paul turns to the Gentile Christians in Rome. He warns them not to allow their membership in the body of Christ to be an occasion for boasting: You are not the tree from which unfaithfulness has caused Jewish branches to be cut off; you are branches from a wild olive tree that have been grafted onto the cultivated olive tree. You do not support the root of that tree; the root supports you. If unbelief alienated the Jews from God, how much more will your unbelief alienate you from him! On the other hand, if the rejection of unbelieving Jews means gain for the world, how much more will God's full acceptance of them do so! (11:13-24).

This description of God's use of Israel's human failing, on the one hand, and warning to the Gentiles against spiritual pride, on the other, is climaxed by Paul's making known a "mystery." Specifically addressing Gentile believers, he writes:

> Lest you be wise in your own conceits, I want you to understand this mystery, brethren: a hardening has come upon part of Israel, until the full number [*pleroma*] of the Gentiles come in, and so all Israel shall be saved. (11:25-26)

He continues with the extraordinary statement that

> as regards the gospel they are enemies of God, for your sake; but as regards election they are beloved for the sake of their forefathers. For the gifts and call of God are irrevocable. (vv. 28-29)

The Jews had so misunderstood the message of salvation proclaimed by the prophets that when its fulfillment came in Christ, they rejected both the message and the one who was its central content. Thus they became "enemies of God." But this was "for your [the Gentiles'] sake." In the strange combination of seemingly incompatible elements, the unbelief of the Jews and their subsequent rejection are accompanied by an unexpected influx of Gentiles into the church.

The refusal of the Jews to hear Paul and Barnabas in Antioch of Pisidia led to the apostles' watershed declaration, "It was necessary that the word of God should be spoken first to you. Since you thrust it from you, and judge yourselves unworthy of eternal life, behold, we turn to the Gentiles" (Acts 13:46).

The realization of the turning of the tables against them so disturbed many of the Jews that in holy jealousy they turned to Christ and thus returned to God. Israel's contrariness did not undo the election of its patriarchs and of the nation born from them. God did not forsake the work of his hands, but in ways inconceivable to Man showed that his gifts and call are indeed irrevocable.

> Just as you [Gentiles] were once disobedient to God but now have received mercy because of their disobedience, so they [the

> Jews] have now been disobedient in order that by the mercy shown to you they also may receive mercy. For God has consigned all men to disobedience, that he may have mercy upon all. (Rom. 11:30-32)

Small wonder that at this point Paul's description of the process of salvation is overtaken by amazement and doxology:

> O the depth of the riches and wisdom and knowledge of God! How unsearchable are his judgments and how inscrutable his ways! "For who has known the mind of the Lord, or who has been his counselor?" "Or who has given a gift to him that he might be repaid?" For from him and through him and to him are all things. To him be glory for ever. Amen. (11:33-36)

In the context of Romans 9–11 four universals are to be noted. They are (a) the "full number" of the Gentiles will come in; (b) "all Israel" will be saved; (c) God consigns "all men" to disobedience; and (d) that he may have mercy "upon all."

The most striking of these is the "full number" of the Gentiles. The Greek word is *pleroma.* It is also rendered as "fullness" or, as in the New English Bible, "in full strength." These are technically acceptable translations, but they quite fail to convey the atmosphere of plenitude or overflowing fullness conveyed by the Greek word. In the common Greek language *pleroma* connoted the idea of superabundance or immeasurability. This comes to expression in New Testament contexts in which "completeness," "totality," "wholeness" would be the most natural words to describe the matter in question, for example, "from his *pleroma* have we all received, grace upon grace" (John 1:16); "the *pleroma* of the blessing of Christ" (Rom. 15:29); "the earth is the Lord's and the *pleroma* of it" (1 Cor. 10:26); "the church, which is his body, the *pleroma* of him who fills all in all" (Eph. 1:22-23); "for in him the *pleroma* of deity dwells bodily" (Col. 2:9).

The "all" in the other three universalistic references does not have the same overtones, but here context is significant. The words "all Israel shall be saved" stand in stark contrast to the familiar "remnant" of the faithful in the Old Testament. The "all" who are consigned to disobedience are in Reformed exegesis necessarily far more numerous than the "all" on whom God will have mercy. Paul, however, does not make this distinction. At the same time, we may not fail to note Paul's warning to the Gentiles when he speaks of God's kindness to them, "provided you continue in his kindness." And of the Jews he says that "if they do not persist in their unbelief" God has the power to graft in again branches that were cut off because of unbelief (Rom. 11:22-23).

The reader will have observed that a universalistic thrust has characterized many of the pages of this book. That is inherent in the theme of coordinating creation and redemption. God the Redeemer reclaims and restores the work of God the Creator. The grand climax of the work of the Creator was calling into being Man as *imago Dei.* To his stewardship was entrusted the whole of that great product of God's created work, the *vestigia Dei,* the world as "footprints of God." That reclaimed and redeemed world included as its head Man, the image of God.

Does God redeem the entirety of mankind, person for person? Certainly not on this side of eternity. But is the dichotomy of the present dispensation to be characteristic of the age to come? In principle, the answer to this question was set forth in the preceding chapter. But again: person for person? Here other questions arise. Did not God's concern with Israel as his "firstborn" among the nations have saving significance for the nations and peoples of the world during the period of its particularism? Inevitably, the same question must be asked in its own context concerning the church during its pilgrimage from cross to consummation. Does not the saving outreach of Christ in his incarnation, life, cross, resurrection, and ascension have retrospective as well as prospective efficacy? Was he not truly the Son of *Man?*

When we take the image of God concept seriously in its circumspection as well as in its (more wonted) introspection, asking these questions is not only unavoidable, but in fact demanded by the scriptural data. We have seen that these data wholly legitimize the question of the extent of human salvation. But as we have also seen, they do not warrant a univocal answer to the questions which their very character requires us to ask.

On one matter, however, the Bible speaks unequivocally and with great certainty: human history will be brought to a close by an all-encompassing divine judgment from which no one will be exempt. Hebrews 10:26-39 is representative of Scripture as a whole:

> For if we sin deliberately after receiving the knowledge of the truth, there no longer remains a sacrifice for sins, but a fearful prospect of judgment. . . . For we know him who said, "Vengeance is mine, I will repay." And again, "The Lord will judge his people." It is a fearful thing to fall into the hands of the living God. (vv. 26-27, 30-31)

To this, however, a significant reservation must be added.

One day as Jesus was setting out on a journey, a man ran up and knelt before him and asked him, "Good Teacher, what must I do to inherit eternal life?" Jesus said, "You know the commandments," and he recited to him the six commandments of the second table of the law. The man responded, "Teacher, all these I have observed from my youth." Jesus, seeing before him an honorable and sincere man, "loved him, and said to him, 'You lack one thing; go, sell what you have, and give to the poor, and you will have treasure in heaven; and come, follow me.' At that saying his countenance fell, and he went away sorrowful; for he had great possessions."

At this, Jesus looked around and said to his disciples, "How hard it will be for those who have riches to enter the kingdom of God!" This amazed the disciples, so Jesus repeated what he had said, and he added, "It is easier for a camel to go through the eye of a needle than for a rich man to enter the kingdom of God." On hearing this the disciples were "exceedingly astonished, and said to him, 'Then who can be saved?' Jesus looked at them and said, 'With men it is impossible, but not with God; for all things are possible with God' " (Mark 10:17-27).

We face also here, therefore, a mystery. Because of their altogether different contexts, we cannot simply identify Jesus'

"With men it is impossible, but not with God; for all things are possible with God" with the mystery of which Paul speaks in Romans 11:25. We can, however, form some idea of the nature of the mystery in which Man's impossibility is a possibility with God.

Who could even by merest chance have conceived that the hardening of Israel's heart to the gospel would trigger the ingathering of the Gentiles into the church? And who could have foreseen that this ingathering would form the occasion for the salvation of "all Israel"? Such an "impossibility" becoming a reality can have only one response, the response of doxology. Doxology is in some contexts a superseding of reason, not because the occasion for the praise is irrational, but because it exceeds the mind's competence to understand the undeniable reality that has come to confront it.

We therefore await the revelation of God's possibility.